fatalism. Our decisions and choices matter, for good or for ill. Here is clear, logical, biblically informed thought, laced with dashes of humor, which consistently argues the point that God created humankind to make a difference in this world and that with the choices we make, we do—one way or the other. Christian pastors, counselors, teachers, and other leaders will especially appreciate the way Middelmann has dismantled the mantra of misguided and ill-informed people who retreat to the opium of 'God has a plan for my life,' when tragedy or hardship strike one's life. God does clearly have a plan for our lives. It is called faithfulness. *Neither Necessary nor Inevitable* is about the importance of making such choices, not only for ourselves, but for the world over which God has given us dominion."

—FRED R. ANDERSON
PASTOR, MADISON AVENUE PRESBYTERIAN CHURCH,
NEW YORK CITY

Neither Necessary nor Inevitable

Neither Necessary nor Inevitable

"History Needn't Have Been Like That"

UDO W. MIDDELMANN

WIPF & STOCK · Eugene, Oregon

NEITHER NECESSARY NOR INEVITABLE
"History Needn't Have Been Like That"

Copyright © 2011 Udo W. Middelmann. All rights reserved. Except for brief quotations in critical publications or reviews, no part of this book may be reproduced in any manner without prior written permission from the publisher. Write: Permissions, Wipf and Stock Publishers, 199 W. 8th Ave., Suite 3, Eugene, OR 97401.

Wipf & Stock
An Imprint of Wipf and Stock Publishers
199 W. 8th Ave., Suite 3
Eugene, OR 97401
www.wipfandstock.com

ISBN 13: 978-1-61097-413-4

Manufactured in the U.S.A.

All scripture quotations, unless otherwise indicated, are taken from the Holy Bible, New International Version®, NIV®. Copyright ©1973, 1978, 1984 by Biblica, Inc.™ Used by permission of Zondervan. All rights reserved worldwide.

"History Needn't Have Been Like That", from James, *Cultural Amnesia*, page 15.

. . . and now there are nine of them, grand children each:

Alexandre, Philippe, Benjamin, Claire
Gaston
Talia, Seraphine
Gabriela, Maximilien

Your lives are evidence of our significance in history,
the results of choices made.

Together with any grandchildren who are yet unborn, know that
we each cause ripples on water and create bends in the road,
because history is neither smooth nor straight, neither necessary
nor inevitable. Much is conditioned on what we do, or fail to do.

Contents

Preface xiii
Introduction   No Right Side of History
   (Recorded History is a Story,
   Real History a Chaos) xix

Chapter 1   How It All Happened? 1
Chapter 2   The Reflection of Nature in Cultures 24
Chapter 3   The Weight of Significance 43
Chapter 4   Weighty Consequences of Our Choices 84
Chapter 5   History in the Seat of the Accused 108

Bibliography 127

Preface

THE DESIRE to have someone or something outside of and prior to us be responsible is perhaps an expression of our wish to be under the wings of a bigger, older, more encompassing "thing," power, or person. We could then escape responsibility in our existential loneliness and experience less discomfort in the problematic world we inherited, but did not make. The attachment would give us a home, explain the seemingly necessary course of past events and excuse us for any mistakes our own choices may turn out to be. That way, none of us would be guilty of history in the past and all of us could continue it and could still blame the past for it.

Looking about we make a curious observation. Our generation has greater freedoms in the way we live our lives, work and study, adopt fewer communal norms, seek wider possibilities of self-expression, and explore cultural relativism. Such colorful things as going ethnic in clothes, food, and family life easily abolish the last ties to our past.

At the same time we look back somewhat anxiously to find an explanation for the way we turned out, what made us the persons we are. With weakened family and cultural ties—frequently due to broken homes and faint confidence in one's philosophical roots—more people today seek the assistance of psychologists and serious genetic research to tell them why they turned out to be who they are. Buying patterns, relationships, religious faith, and political priorities are increasingly more tied to an assumed quasi-mechanical influence on the brain from birth, early childhood educational experiences, various traumas, and the influence of Hollywood movies.

Whatever the notes, the music is composed by reducing all present acts to inevitable influences. That is a modern variant of old pagan determinism, where gods and fates, where the stars in the firmament, where destiny arranges all without leaving anything to choice or chance. More recently we find this notion of a seamless cloth of push-and-shove relationships in Hegel's view of history, later adapted by Marx as the inevitable scientific progress through class struggles to a new humanity. One controlling principle directs all events in history, whether genetics, energy, or god. Today, we hear the phrase that someone is on the right (or wrong) side of history, as if history were a set program, an inevitable advance, a sequence of events that cannot be messed up or become untidy.

For me this rings the bells of a familiar tune. Oneness, unity, harmony, and control, to remove the unexpected, the unnecessary, and the inevitable, in search of a tidy world, is characteristic of Eastern religions, Islam, traditionalism, and secular utopian totalitarianism. Plato had his static universals and wrote against the untidy influences of artists and poets. Hitler made his appeal to Germanic Nationalism and Stalin to the abstraction of Internationalism and a new mankind.

All the cows in the field across from my house will return home to their stable in the evening. But people are in their personal essence less tidy, unpredictable, surprisingly creative, and also disappointing. They are significant and create history. There is a crooked timber of humanity, as Kant said and as Isaiah Berlin referred to it. That is part of the glory of human beings and the foundation of their freedom and our hope, in the midst of much evil, for better solutions to pressing problems in society, the political arena, and the environment, than having to wait for history to deliver them.

For history delivers neither problems nor solutions! History just happens, including when very little happens at all, because the worldviews of repetition, taught and imposed by social systems and religious views, humiliate and fail to nourish human beings in their minds and suspect, fear, and oppose their complaint and initiative. We can think of the waste of human potential in many cultures, where one half the population's minds and abilities, those of women, are squashed, and their contribution to everyone is religiously limited to serving their men and bearing their children.

What a contrast here to Jewish thought and Christianity, where events, inventions, art, and moral courage are identified by the names of responsible individuals, not by historic sequence or as a moment on an impersonal timeline. Common to both propositions is the understanding that the human being is made in the image of the creator to be creative him- and herself. There are several actors on the stage of history, and nothing is happening by some enforced necessity or inevitability. The Bible frees people from the prison of a past determinant of all choices, events, and occurrences. People can and must, after the fall, argue with God, themselves, and circumstances, lest history runs a course without repentance, innovation and participation.

There is a thread running through all my books, which ties them loosely together around the recognition that thought, words, and decision are essential to being human. They express human significance through ideas and actions. History is not a simple record of what happened, but the result of choices made, thoughts externalized, and options considered. There is nothing necessary or inevitable about it.

Pro-Existence (Downers Grove, IL: InterVarsity, 1974) addressed a generation which saw work as destructive and spontaneity as more honest. They had turned their backs on their parent's lives and sought an independence from the requirements of an objective world. The book suggests that work is not a curse, but the central expression of ideas into the external world by human beings with mandates from God to discover, shape, and be responsible for a rich life for every person.

The Market-Driven Church (Wheaton, IL: Crossway, 2004) brought out what the teaching of the Bible had done to change a violent and pagan continent of Europe into something more humane, compassionate, lawful, and creative. The church's work had humanized somewhat the common and intellectual life when Rome had left things untidy. Yet, what we have in modern Christianity has weakened the substance by turning the Bible's teaching into a quarry for mostly personal faith, private opinion, and irrational satisfaction.

The Innocence of God (Colorado Springs: Authentic/STL, 2007) frees God from the accusation of his failure, and even his evil intent, after the horrors of the twentieth century. Many Europeans have only heard of the link between God's being and history and therefore reject God on moral and intellectual grounds. The book also sets God apart from the association between tragic and terrible events, both personal and on the larger stage of history, and God's sovereign will, purpose, and intentions. This has become a favorite among believing Christians, though what they believe about God doing such things according to his plan all along has nothing to do with the God of the Bible. For that God agonizes, is frustrated, weeps, and is furious about what evil people do and say and intervenes to set things and ideas right.

In *Christianity vs. Fatalistic Religions in the War against Poverty* (Colorado Springs: Authentic/STL, 2008) I show how different non-Christian worldviews turn out to be faulty when you compare them to the form and requirements of the real world. Fatalistic religions impose a view that humiliates each person, insults their unique personality, and requires them to become something less than human. They require conformity, repetition, and acceptance without allowing persons to think through and try alternatives more noble to the human person. They in fact teach that whatever is was meant to be, has always been, and must not be changed. It leads to great suffering, puts no thought in people's mind and heart and little food into their mouths. The real poverty is one of spirit and mind and social customs, not a lack of resources.

The contribution of Jewish and Christian biblical thought in practice built up an island of relative sanity and concern for human beings in a sea of essentially disrespectful religious and intellectual sludge. Unless each generation constantly maintains that view of Man and the world under the God of the Bible, that island will sink into the surrounding attitudes and practices. To see all events in life as determined, planned, willed, and purposed by a higher authority joins everyone else in their deterministic perspective, where history is necessary and inevitable.

In the present book I want to show our responsibility to seek wisdom, foresight, and circumspection in the choices we face every day. The choice to act or to abstain is equally weighty with consequence. We have memories of the increasing influence of biblical thought on politics, economics, law, the sciences, and the concern for human rights and the environment. Our responsibility at this time is, among other things, to see that future generations will not be left with only a memory of our failing to pass on the explanations of those insights from the Bible.

Jehovah saw human history in need of prophets to interfere and to call people back to moral responsibility. Jesus saw history in need of opposition to the religious and secular authorities, to the blindness of people and the unfairness of life in a fallen world. Where Plato in his *Timaeus* dialogue has a closed firmament as final horizon, Jesus restores sight to the blind man Bartimaeus, so that he can see the real foundation of life in the God of heaven.

History is then neither a necessary program nor an inevitable sequence of events. It is up to each of us what we choose and do.

Gryon, May 2011

Introduction

No Right Side of History (Recorded History is a Story, Real History a Chaos)

IF THEY had made different choices, 146 young women could have lived out their lives as they had hoped. There was no need for it, no divine appointment, no ring of fate or natural source or personal destiny. From greed and mistrust a situation was created that ended tragically simply because the doors had been locked to prevent unscheduled bathroom breaks. It was neither necessary nor inevitable.

Every year soon after the unnecessary tragedy of 1911, a memorial service has been held on Greene Street off Washington Square in New York City.[1] On March 25 that year all 146 women and men died in the great fire there. Since then their names are read every year, one by one, and a fire truck with a raised ladder, but raised only so far, pays tribute—a reminder of a rescue effort that fell tragically short.

In 2011 it will be one hundred years since a fire at the Triangle Shirtwaist factory took the lives of garment work-

---

1. *Choosing Not to Forget What Is Painful to Recall* by Clyde Haberman, NY Times March 25, 2010.

ers—most of them women, most of them Jewish and Italian immigrants, most of them heartbreakingly young.

The flames that engulfed the factory, on the top three floors of a building that still stands on that location in the midst of New York University, was the most cataclysmic disaster to befall a New York workplace before 2001. But even the attacks of September 11 have not diminished Triangle's central place in the consciousness of an oft-wounded city.

There were accounts of how the many low-paid seamstresses who made ladies' blouses—shirtwaists—were trapped in the blaze. How locked doors prevented many from fleeing to safety. How the firefighters' tallest ladder reached only to the sixth floor, well below workers trying to stave off death two, three, and four floors higher. How in desperation—does this sound familiar?—many jumped to their deaths.

There were speeches from labor leaders about how the disaster led to tougher safety regulations but also about how much remains undone. Locking in workers? Last month, in an echo of Triangle, twenty-one workers in Bangladesh died in a fire at a garment factory with locked exits.

And there was the mournful tolling of a firehouse bell, each ring accompanying a name, each name capturing a soul: Lizzie Adler, Rosina Cirrito, Yetta Goldstein, Gaetana Midolo, Simie Wisotsky, and, every now and then, Unidentified Woman or Unidentified Man.

Around the account of the Triangle Fire revolves a civic memory because it has clear constituencies. It is part of the Italian-American narrative and, arguably even more so, of Jewish-American history. But there is more to it, said

David Von Drehle, the author of "Triangle: The Fire That Changed America."

Triangle "speaks to large trends—the immigrant story, the progressive political story, the labor movement story, and the women's rights story," Mr. Von Drehle said. "It's illustrative of current living issues."

Others visit the places where each of the 146 victims lived, mostly in the East Village and on the Lower East Side. At those locations, on the pavement, they chalk in the names and ages of those who died. "It's the idea of making communal memory visible," Ms. Sergel, a filmmaker, said, describing it as "a different kind of power." "It's not permanent," she said. "It washes away. But you know what? It's going to come back next year."

Five hundred years before, William Shakespeare had Horatio close the play of *Hamlet* with these fitting lines:

> ... give order that these bodies
> High on a stage be placed to the view;
> And let me speak to the yet unknowing world
> How these things came about: so shall you hear
> Of carnal, bloody, and unnatural acts,
> Of accidental judgments, casual slaughters,
> Of deaths put on by cunning and forced cause,
> And, in this upshot, purposes mistook
> Fall'n on the inventors' reads: all this can I
> Truly deliver ...
> ... Let this same be presently perform'd,
> Even while men's minds are wild;
> lest more mischance
> On plots and errors, happen.

Far from the notion of a destiny, a fate, or God controlling all events, events in the past remind us vividly that history is something that could have gone differently: fires could have been prevented, the doors left unlocked, escapes made accessible into the higher floors and onto neighboring roofs. People's actions, like Hamlet's rage over the usurpation of his father's throne and bed by wicked treachery and murder, were not ordained and thus excusable, inevitable, or in the predictable run of events.

So much of what is now history did not need to happen that way. We are all caught up in what went before. That cannot be changed. But we should also recognize that through our choices we give shape to history. We inherit a situation, but there is no need to let it continue without interference on our part. Neither fate nor the will of God determine what authentic choice we can make.

Alone for that reason, we can be blamed or praised, and later remembered for the hurt we caused or the benefit we brought freely into existence. Memorials remind us of the heroism of individuals and the preventability of many disasters. We need to distinguish between natural—and hence unavoidable—and man-made tragedies. We shall reduce the former gradually through greater insight and chosen effort. About the latter, let human cruelty "high on a stage be placed to view," and teach us lessons to avoid a repetition.

History is not a case of trying to figure out the *what if* riddles of life. There is no way to know the course and consequences of hypothetical decisions. What if you had done another thing, made another choice, stopped in your tracks, put away your whim or first impression: all that is the stuff of novels, of dreams, and of imagination. There is no history to that, because the *what if* never took on form, since it was precisely not carried out. We must leave that behind. Instead, we need to see that once real choices have been made their consequences are real, whichever choice was made.

The American author John Irving (*Ciderhouse Rules*, *The World According to Garp*, *A Prayer for Owen Meany*, and *Last Night in Twisted River*) tells us that he always knows the end of his novels down to the last line in the final paragraph before he starts to write them. He writes from the "finale" and constructs the way characters and circumstances lead up to it. He knows the conclusion and takes us there in a manner that seems inevitable. It is a marvelous way to write a story, but it cannot be done for history. History records things that unrolled from the front, from sovereign choices with a future outcome often not known. History is neither made up of hypothetical situations nor of necessary choices into which personages are pressed by some higher purpose. Instead, as we shall suggest, history is a record of the things that did take place, but did not necessarily have to.

That is also the biblical perspective. God created a real world, but left it deliberately unfinished. It was perfect, but neither complete nor fixed in time. Man, male and female, the creature made in God's image to think, create, choose, imagine, was mandated to add to, alter, and have dominion day after day over creation, firstly, and, secondly, his own choices. That is the will of God, the purpose of creation: Man should be a human being and make history!

And what a success it was and is. I have never met a non-human human being.

The Jewish and Christian Scripture tell us about the creation of real history. Both communities exist because of the constant reference to historical reality. Their concern revolves around events in real time and space brought about by choices of God and/or people. Choices have necessary and inevitable consequences in a rational and temporal creation and thereby set the stage for further choices. There is much dynamic interplay between God and Man (and Angels) in, at first, mutual admiration. After the Fall of Man, the interplay became more laborious, untidy, and burdensome. As sin increased, God gave additional mandates to fight for life, justice, and hope in a world now marked by death, unfairness, and despair.

All that takes place now in a dynamic history of frustrated efforts by God and stupid evasions by Man, of promises neglected and conditions violated. At all times and in real history before God and Man, the various choices and their consequences add complexity. As the results are unnecessary and avoidable, they can be judged morally as well as observed factually.

I want to show you the exceptional perspective of the worldview that produced a culture more respectful of human beings than what modern secular and traditional religious views propose.

The heart of Marxist materialism was the belief that big matter in the universe (like the stars, sun, and moon) and the material conditions of people's lives (like their wealth and poverty, living conditions, and degree of health) determined their behavior along the inevitable process of a history with quasi-divine force and capabilities. We shall see how the Bible frees us from a closed destiny and expects us to reform history.

Such a dynamic is not seen or taught in most religions. It is denied wherever someone suggests that everything is already the way it has to be, either by material forces or by divine will. In that case all reality follows one chain of necessary events in a unity of purpose. All religions in East and West teach that invariably. Allah, Buddha, religious tribal traditions, and Hegel and modern naturalistic science assume a closed system of necessary destinies, of an invariable power, of an impersonal unity of Being. Religions tempt people to subordinate all events to a material logic or a master's dominion.

In the first chapter I shall lay out the burden and delights of the larger circle of our life. With our eyes we see the immediate, but our mental curiosity inquires into the material and personal factors that brought about the present. With our minds, we see a larger world of past choices that have contributed to our untidy, often disturbing experiences, like a stone thrown into a pond causes a sequence of ripples across a wide surface. The Bible shines on that surface and into the shadows of the past.

The second chapter presents the difference in life's practices without the Bible, when nature gives shape to culture, when the human is a victim rather than a skillful master over circumstances. Most painful is the obligatory acceptance of resignation and repetition, where Jewish and Christian views call people to be seekers, innovators, and inventors to give shape to history. I give illustrations from history to show the practical and fruitful applications of powerful ideas.

The third chapter illustrates the biblical view of human and divine significance in an unfinished creation with an open history. Using biblical personages and situations, I show that history could easily have gone another way, not because of thrown dice, or the will of God, or nature's whims, but alone because of the true significance of personal choices. Cain, Abraham, Joseph's brothers, David and Mary et al. made choices as real people, and God as God. Decisions affect whole cultures for generations after![2] We bear a burden of necessary and inevitable effects from earlier causes, but we also exercise dominion over our minds and bodies, places, and times from here on forward.

The fourth chapter lays out the many philosophical, political/social, and theological efforts to deny the perplexing, untidy, and unfinished reality of reality, of which the crooked timber of humanity (Isaiah Berlin) is a central part. System thinking, a natural program, the will of God, the orderliness of the cosmos are drawn on to suggest the rightfulness of the normal. It contradicts the effort of God in Christ to fight what is in fact abnormal, wrong, evil, and marked by death in any of its forms. The Heavenly Father of the Bible shares no home with an impersonal "Mother Nature." Plato's *Timaeus* saw the orderly heavens closed; Jesus made the blind man Bar-timaeus (Son-of-Timaeus) see.[3]

The fifth chapter lays out how the biblical understanding of life frames freedom with responsibility. That coupling stands in contrast to the temptations at all times to force all

---

2. Consider *Then Everything Changed: Stunning Alternate Histories of American Politics,* by Jeff Greenfield (New York: Putnam, 2011), a political journalist with familiarity to recent politics. While some may see here the playfulness with fate, I see it as evidence of the real significance of choices: It is not so much *what if* as *now that* . . .

3. Mark 10:46–52.

events and people into a programmatic, established order. The picture of a tidy world is attractive and has its roots in Athens, away from Jerusalem. Greece seeded ideas that for centuries grew into utopian visions of achievable perfection through politics and religion and by an embrace of nature as normal. These are attempts to impose perfection on the creative and therefore open, untidy, unpredictable reality of human existence. What is essentially human is each time sacrificed, for it is untidy. The God of the Bible informs, loves, exhorts, argues, pleads, and delights. In that perspective, the calling of each human being to be God's agent in the world, to act intelligently on sound moral foundations, undergirds the command to love God with heart, mind, soul, and strength, and also each neighbor, made as much in his image as ourselves.

Chapter 1

How It All Happened?

All of us expect an explanation eventually. It is not enough to know that something happened. That is a question about facts. In our rich Western tradition and under the influence of the historical religions of Judaism and Christianity, we also want to know why it happened and possibly who did it. Our minds transcend the present and seek links to past decisions. We live in the present, but the present had a past we want to know about. Our interest is focused on more than the facts, the statistics. We also seek to understand reasons for them. Such questions crawl up the causal links to establish the moral responsibility behind the event.

We keep looking, asking; we turn pages, compare, and evaluate. We peer into nooks and crannies to discover the key that would unlock books or boxes that would explain much and thereby satisfy our curiosity, our anxiety, and our sense that something is not resolved.

I do not mean solutions only to mystery novels or answers to, "Who did it?" No, I mean that endless questioning that accompanied us from early childhood when we first began to discover things in the real world. We began to notice not only a variety of impressions, faces, voices, and means of satisfying our needs without at first discerning them consciously. Happily our parents knew or, with patience and imagination, guessed what these were and then found ways to still our complaint, our hunger and pain, ways to remove our loneliness or just to deal with our wetness.

We also began to notice the details of the real world and how it functioned. Different material objects, not always harmless, were put into the mouth, held between fingers, moved, lost, discovered, then treasured or discarded.

We discovered links between "before and after," "here and there," and words and objects as our minds grew to realize temporal and spacial extensions. We learned to notice differences between "mine and yours" as well as "real and imaginary." And in this manner our development took in ever larger shapes of the real world by means of increasing facility with words, of physical coordination, and of a developing awareness of identity, of the self. We became aware of moral distinctions, the power to understand and to manipulate situations and people, as well as of how many more areas of life existed about which we possibly knew very little.

All along, from the physical and emotional curiosity of a baby, through those magic years of becoming aware of one's own magic powers,[1] into the teenage years, and beyond to adulthood, we have found that questioning is a natural approach of human beings to an unknown world. Getting answers was a way of gaining power over the wild things out there, at least to diminish somewhat the size and scope of the "known unknowns and the unknown unknowns."[2] That

1. See Selma H. Fraiberg, *The Magic Years: Understanding and Handling the Problems of Early Childhood* (New York: Scribner, 1959).

2. No joke, but a fitting term for much more than what was the concern of former Secretary of Defense Donald Rumsfeld, who

How It All Happened? 3

world holds us and yet is outside of us at the same time. It makes sense in many areas, yet is full of danger. It presents us with the freedom of choices but then burdens us with the weight of consequences—our own after us and those that were already handed down from previous generations. And when we look at the reality we were born into, we wonder why it had to come about that way or whether it could not have been otherwise.

In practice we assume that we can make a difference. We learn things to improve the skills we need, for instance, to read what others have published for us so that we might learn and benefit from it. We learn math to be more accurate in our dealings with quantities, measures, and the change from our purchases. Geography situates us in the world and tells us where, why, and how other people cope, live, and trade. Religion teaches us about their beliefs about life, meaning, and social customs. It gives us their explanation of how they see the original and final truth of the universe with their own eyes. Foreign languages allow us to get closer and into the minds of people further away, their ideas, their experiences, and how they cope with the real world, real pain, and real neighbors. History locates us in time. It gives us a background, the effects of choices, underlying ideas, and views, and their consequences.

All these subjects alert us to greater possibilities and greater failures in the history of the human race. What we learn encourages and warns us. It can lead to discouragement and envy, even depression, when we realize, quite soon, how easy it is to make bad choices. Sometimes it seems that we can't help ourselves from lack of enough prior

---

brought it into public discourse.

insight. At other times we make them to escape the perils surrounding us and to resist the temptations that lure us.

But knowledge also enables us to make honorable and healthy choices with greater wisdom. Then they encourage, stimulate competition for increased competence in various fields. We realize then that we are not totally locked into the familiar routine. A wider insight into human diversity challenges our tribalism and nationalistic hyperbole, just like travel and trade open closed minds and limited goals.

The power to shape our lives in some substantial measure can be as terrifying as it is liberating.

That wider insight allows us to stand on the shoulders, so to speak, of those who worked before us, in order to see further ahead and broader afield. We are grateful that not every generation or every individual has to start from scratch. What we learn answers some of the questions we had (or should have had) to understand the shape and nature of reality, where we have come from and where we need to go. We do not only want to improve our professional chances but also our way of looking at life and "doing it well."

The combination of both interests—to meet both the factual skills requirement for the ability to be a craftsman of your life as well as the moral/ethical evaluation for the ability to make wise choices—is essential for our personal satisfaction now and in the future. Our own children in the next generation will review us and, when needed, take us to task.

For when we ask whether things really had to happen the way they did for us, or when we realize that history is a record of things that did not need to happen in the way they did, we realize that the accusation about bad choices in the past will one day also stand against us. "What did you do in the war, the great recession, the tech or the real estate bubble, Dad?" These are only a few of the myriad questions we will be asked by our children. They may want to accuse us, their parents, of leaving for them all the difficulties they will then face. They may well fail to see the prior circumstantial conditions created by an earlier generation that made some outcomes irreparable or even inevitable for the next. But they are correct to express their frustration over things in which a different choice by us would have produced a more favorable situation for them.

Put yourself into their shoes, into their moment of (yet future) history and make a list of questions that you would (then) ask about the mess each generation (that would be ours, now!) leaves behind for others to address and to attempt to clean up!

We will always wonder whether what has happened was unavoidable, necessary, determined, in the nature of things and people, God's will in one way or another, or whether in fact things have turned out in a manner that was not necessary. In which case we should well ask why people made such choices, why they did not ask questions about their lives, context, and situation, to find better answers and have history go in another direction. Just as missing an exit on the turnpike may take you far away, a small shift at some point may have dramatic consequences down the road.

FREEDOM AS BURDEN AND DELIVERANCE

In addition to our natural curiosity as human beings, we also inherit a particular cultural context, a view of reality, of human significance, and of the power to make choices.

Our specific cultural context was born out of the Jewish and Christian encouragement to search for wider explanations. While the beginning of each person anywhere in the world is identical in terms of our humanity, our way of exhibiting our human nature—how we look at life around us—differs widely. We shall consider some of those differences and their origins in the world of people's ideas later on. For now we must realize that the cultural context of which we are heirs—the view of Human life and the freedom of the mind and thought—is found in Jewish and Christian ideas rooted in the Bible, even though religious authorities have often suppressed such inquiry.

The support for inquiries from the Bible, what makes us "protest" the limits of our knowledge, has many sources. Perhaps foremost is the fact that God created a knowable world, in which we can see God's mind, imagination, and power exhibited. But we also raise questions, because life in that world is not safe. It is fragile, prone to pain and certain death, and we need to know whether that is part of the design or whether a flaw crept into it later: in the Bible we are told that there has been a fall with cosmic effects, that nature also is no longer what God had made it to be.

We seek to understand our moral obligations to interfere in the workings of society and nature in order to fulfill the demands of justice, love, and compassion. Jews and Christians do not have instructions to lie low, to accept, and to submit to what is a consequence of natural conditions or prior human folly. Far from being in any form fatalistic, we are called to resist evil, to feed the hungry, to argue with authorities, and to start a new chain of beneficial effects from the choices we initiate.

Persistent questioning through all levels of human development assumes that answers can be found eventually. Only a world of recognizable behavior or patterns, where everything functions "according to its kind," gives you a reason for that and lets you continue. A world of random events, obvious contradictions, mischievous forces, or unsteady general patterns frustrates such a search for explanations. Insight in that kind of a world can only ever account for the one present event. From it alone we cannot discover a reliable source of wisdom for future ones. A fact is noticed and described, but without a larger network of reliable laws, it becomes incidental, easily the subject of a painting by Rene Magritte.

The Bible lays a framework for a steady, defined reality in two areas: The definite character of God and the world of things and people that produce "after their kind": fruit trees produce their fruit, animals mate and give birth to their young, and human beings only ever conceive ideas with their minds and other human beings with their bodies. It is in the nature of animals and things to function according to their template. It is in the nature of human beings to make choices.

Ours is a world of law, of cause and effect, not of haphazard occurrences. In a lawful reality, things can be discovered and then used, because essentially they will not change merely because of the weather or the times or because the geography has changed. Things affect each other, there is interplay of factors, but they in themselves remain as they are and always have been. Water always runs downhill!

That is the view the Bible presents from the outset. Under its instruction and with its declarations, which confirm our observations, our culture has done amazingly well. We have been able to recognize real problems, contradictions, and violations, where otherwise, and without reference to the laws of nature (both the nature of things and the nature of people), we would be confronted only with variations of particular events, things, and people, without any possibility to speak of any normality. The insight into a basic lawfulness alone makes it possible for us to become aware of aberrations. Only when we recognize problems will questions arise about possible and necessary solutions. Variations of single normal occurrences merely appear as isolated and disjointed experiences outside of a moral framework.

The Bible nurtured our cultural context. It admits both form and freedom. The form is found in a created world of lawful, definable specifics and repetitive processes. In addition, there is true freedom found in the openness of activities by personages, both God and the human being, who bears the image of God. God created an orderly but unfinished world. In it he gave Man mandates to create, to investigate, to work, and to love, with the consequence that no day would be a mere repetition of the previous one. History was not locked in the mind of God, but open to his continuing creation and participation. God's all encompassing knowledge did not make all events or choices by the creature inevitable. Adam and Eve would not only freely give names to animals. They would also have the babies they chose to have, subdue the earth, and have dominion over themselves, over the world around them, and over what they would decide to do in genuine creativity.

Any obedience that was part of the arrangement of creatures under the Creator was centered on loving God and believing him. They were to show their love by doing what they were made to do: that is to be human beings and to love and find pleasure in God, each other, and creation. They would manifest this love by not doing the one thing they were commanded to abstain from. The forbidden fruit of the tree was like a tripwire to sound the alarm, when they chose to treat God with indifference.

In terms of our reflection of whether history was a divine program or whether things did not have to turn out the way they did, the Bible indicates clearly that Man's choices would have multiplying and diversifying consequences in a history much fuller than it was at the end of six days of Creation.

THE ALWAYS SURPRISING SEQUENCE OF HISTORICAL EVENTS.

It is interesting that the Bible tells us of a sequential creation by God over six distinct periods of time. He did not make all things at once to give them a shape that they would then maintain forever. Creation and alteration were both part of the way in which God proceeded. Each new period of time God finishes another project of increasing detail. He looks at what he has made and is pleased with it. It corresponds to what he had had in mind, and it is very good. A new page of continuous history is, so to speak, turned after each creative choice.

And for Man, God had in mind that we would continue to create beyond the day of God's rest. We would not merely admire what is, but add to it, change it, explore and discover it, give it distinct names: from an animal to a human partner, from a loving sexual relationship, for which God gave no prescription, to conceiving children in extension of the unity of a marriage between a male and a female.

Our view of the human role in history is not limited to these indications in the Creation account. The entire Bible is a record in many styles, of people and events, generation after generation, through wars and in peace, a collection of the best and the worst of human realities. God is always present, always just, compassionate, and merciful in relation to people in history, through interventions by the words of prophets, through miraculous acts, and by personally appearing at times, as when he came for lunch with Abraham.[3]

Here we find the intellectual and cultural foundation for our sustained mentality of discovery. We do not rest until we find what makes some sense. We question, look for sources, information. We address other people who perhaps know more, who have lived longer, who might remember other times. We do not let life roll by without wondering, What would happen if . . . ?

For good reasons, and from multiple confirmations, we expect answers to our questions. We find that the universe, more than just the world of our daily experience, coheres amazingly well. It is a rational world, and rationality, careful inquiry, critical examination, and peer review of our findings help us define what is true. Then we check it out and refine our perception where required.

---

3. Gen 18:1–8.

The rational criteria of investigation are not arbitrary but are themselves demanded by the regularity of natural occurrences, by the interaction of studied insights from a multitude of angles, by the cross relations between the details under investigation that contribute to what has been recognized as a valid method to reach knowledge (science).

Like yarn spun from threads, slowly gathered knowledge from many corners allows us to weave a cloth with which to dress our otherwise naked ignorance. It may not all fit together well, but we are no longer bare and exposed to a cruel and painful reality.

Things, events, and much of the rest make sense most of the time. Where we come across the unexpected, we human beings can generally probe further and find an explanation sooner or later. In fact we look for further insights not only to understand the big things, but also to expose the workings "behind" the visible.

THE PUZZLE OF REAL PEOPLE

People, and that includes all of us, are more difficult to figure out. Together with following a pattern in our biology, it is in our nature to make choices. We can be quite original and start things that have no further link backwards than to a human being's use of his or her ability to make a choice, to decide. Of course we do not want to close down the inquiry at that point. We will always try to understand reasons for the choice. Are there natural factors that weigh on our conscience and consciousness, so that what is considered a choice is, in reality, at least in part, already somewhat affected by external circumstances?

Illness, frustration, depression, upbringing, and other such physical and emotional weights easily diminish our free exercise of the mind to make a choice. The degree of our independence to make choices free from such burdens external to the will would only be known fully by God. Scripture hints at that when it treats responsibility with great care and respects as real the different factors considered for diminishing accountability in criminal cases. Both the demand for two credible witnesses and the command against bearing false must be kept in mind. In addition the systems of courts of appeals, as demonstrated in Numbers 15 in relation to the man caught gathering wood on the Sabbath, acknowledges the difficulty in establishing exact accountability for each individual.

But there remains, beyond all unavoidable factors from prior powerful influences, something else that points to human choice-makers and their significance. This is assumed in every culture that uses evaluative language and has a refined system of laws. We discuss personal dignity or human rights, which suppose a unique personal being, a free agent, a choice-maker who is responsible. A person is able and obligated to give a response to whomever about why he or she decided something they claim to be their original creation. It flows from their will, their more or less de-liberate ("rendered free") originality. Were it not so, we would have to eliminate all words with moral content and could not place meaning, intent, and purpose into anyone's work, speech, or acts.

In a world where everything is necessary and inevitable there remains no room for either praise or blame on the basis of a person's actions or the response given. All language would be descriptive, not prescriptive, factual, not persuading.

The Bible uses words with moral content widely. Human significance is at all times affirmed. The most basic and central designation of what a human being is, before any limitation is established, is that Man is "in the Image of God." That is a treasure that no sin or fall or evil can take away. It is confirmed before and after the Fall of Adam.[4] Nothing has changed in that fundamental definition of what a human being is. Man, male and female, is equally made in the image of God. As bearer of God's image, Man is creative, makes choices, and affects God's entire world in fulfillment of the mandates God gave us: Have dominion, love your neighbor as yourself, name the animals, and have babies. Do all that in love and enjoyment of God with all your heart, mind, soul, and strength.

Most other cultures do not employ terms of honest praise as centrally as terms of guilt in their perception of the individual. They see each person caught in a web of interlocking forces. Fates, spirits, gods, and cosmic energy forces surround them so tightly that the person is merely driven by the program embraced by his or her faith. He or she is not responsible for anything, for better or for worse, is without significance, meriting neither blame nor praise. He is always a victim. Here the person is light like a leaf on the surface of a river. He is never heavy like a stone that causes ripples or a log that interrupts or diverts the flow of things.

With the biblical understanding, I want to deliberately paint such a forceful contrast to the view in other cultures of people and the things of nature. According to such views, both Man and things function lawfully according to a natural or spiritual program, down to the smallest atoms and molecules.

4. Gen 1:26, 9:6.

By contrast, according to the Bible and our experience, only *things* are expected to do, each time and anywhere in the world, what they do. In nature everything was made "according to its kind." Everything will at all times fulfill what it was made to do: Apples will grow on apple trees, cows will calve, clouds will bring rain, and water will always run downhill. Even Heisenberg's indeterminacy principle, or the more recent chaos theory, describes everything in relation to a steady universe and fixed values—the speed of light, for example. Undetermined are the limited human means of observation. Indeterminacy does not suggest a fundamental shake-up of our understanding about and our operations within a regular universe.

People alone remain an open secret, a surprise, for better and for worse, a pain and a relief. When they were made "according to their kind," it was with the openness of genuine and often original choices.

There are all kinds of surprises in our experiences. Life for us is more "alive" that way. We know a lot, but certainly not everything. We have open minds, a willingness to be humbled in our relative ignorance, and hopefully, also an artistic, inventive attitude towards the things we do not yet understand. Without that, our interest would be dull, the questions we ask too narrow, our expectations too limited. There would be no stimulation for and satisfaction from the arts and sciences.

Surprises of discovery help us to be somewhat dissatisfied with what we know so far. They energize further searches. They get us out of the rut of the known, which Daniel Boorstin decries when he writes that "the greatest obstacle to discovery is not ignorance—it is the illusion of knowledge".[5] Boorstin repeats that proposition in other works as well. "There has been no greater obstacle to (man's) learning than the stock of accumulated learning that he has made for himself with his illusions of knowledge"[6], and then refers to Francis Bacon's suggestions that these illusions are "idols which beset man's minds".[7]

We should, therefore, keep on looking further and press on because we are conscious of not ever knowing everything.

A central puzzle, and at times a great surprise, is our own existence and how it fits into the course of events. Once we recognize that we are here, we wonder about history and our part in it: what we have received from it, how it has shaped us, and how we continue it. This involves questions of identity, purpose, and significance. It involves a search to understand the things that happen to us, why good things happen to average people and bad things to others. Why is so much of the world so messed up? If everything in nature is in fact lawful, nothing should be out of line. But if people create surprises, why am I the one who has to face and often

---

5. Boorstin, *The Discoverers*, xv. Boorstin adds on page 86: "The great obstacle to discover the shape of the earth was not ignorance, but the illusion of knowledge."

6. Boorstin, *The Seekers*, 155.

7. Bacon, *Novum Organum*. He uses aphorisms to describe as idols, or illusions, impediments of various kinds that interfere with the process of clear human reasoning. Aphorism xxxvii (40): "The idols and false notions which have got hold on man's intellects and are now profoundly rooted in them, not only block their minds so that it is difficult for truth to gain access, but even when access has been granted and allowed, they will once again, in the very renewal of the sciences, offer resistance and do mischief unless men are forewarned and arm themselves against them as much as possible."

pay for the consequences of other people's surprising and often unnecessary decisions? There is a sequential rationale to this, but where is the moral consideration?

LIFE FULL OF ARGUMENTS

Look at the question above. Such questions are raised in the Bible, where so many people expected to find solutions, not more problems. But such are also in the Bible where events provoke people to argue with God, with themselves, and others. Do you not have questions about the justice of God when the Flood drowned everyone not safely in the ark: men, women, and children alike? Does everything occur from mere necessity? Are things meant to be and to happen along some gigantic impersonal mechanism or in accordance with an amoral divine sovereign? Is the impersonal natural world the final cause, or is there a god, a demon, or some other spiritual personage who arranges all things and events? Either explanation would fit with that part of our experience that suggests we live in a lawful, rather than a random, context. We would know what is happening and also how it was caused. We would have an underlying formula for the universe, according to which nothing would ever really be out of line. But it would be overall unjust, since it would not consider the reality of personal accountability for each person.

We need to make room for the reality of our own choices and those of others. We are accountable, according to common and legal language, and relational assumptions in our culture, and in the Bible. We are regarded as active, taking initiative for better and for worse. The buck always stops on someone's desk. We accuse the guilty and admire the heroine.

It takes no specific effort to realize that we were all born without having had a say. We did not choose our time, parents, nationality, economic standing, or gender. And yet, now that we are here, we all continue to act into the world around us, alter its shape, and leave behind evidence of our significance, both positive and negative.

Zorro marked his actions with his sword with much dramatic flair. In a parallel way we mark time, less by letting it pass than by burning our name into history by our actions.

None of us is guilty of starting history, yet we all, in diverse ways, continue it. We do not sit on the sideline, like picnickers on the edge of a creek. We step into the water; little waves form around our body and ruffle the surface from here on downriver, and to each shore. We add more than days and years to what becomes history around us. Our ideas and creativity, labor and emotions, a few children perhaps, an article or a poem or a new device, a bent in the political landscape, and here and there perhaps even a solution to a real problem: such waves never cease. Even after our death they speak of our having been and having made a difference.

In some cultural contexts, the image of such a river is used to describe an inevitable history. There, people will not step into it and intercept the quiet flow. Instead the human being is told to be like a leaf, silently carried along wherever the river takes it, causing no ripples and taking no stand.

In our cultural heritage, from biblical Judaism and Christianity, the human being, man, woman, and child, matters. We are considered "a little lower than the angels"[8] but far above impersonal leaves or other parts of nature. We think, have clear and distinct cognitive abilities, and a mentality of inquiry, of doubt. We want to know the power of the river, its direction, the location of its estuary before the water mingles with the ocean. And when we have an idea about these things, we may well want to get back on land by going across the current until we have solid rock under our feet.

At each moment of our lives we ask questions about a larger context, about the connectedness of events, about the past, and into the future. When did the parents meet, where did the parents live, where was I before I was born?

Human beings ask such questions from a sense of transcendence of the moment and a need to have an explanation. We want to know how events hang together, what caused the present situation. The human being is not satisfied merely observing the day. History had a past and will have a future. We want to know what preceded the now and how our choices will affect what will flow. Does my life matter into the next decade? Whose life weighed, literally "mattered," so much that his decisions contributed to the shape of the wider political, economic, and cultural context that we inherited and now have to deal with?

Human beings want to know not only what is, but also why things are that way. The question *what* is a matter of observing, learning to read the signs, and counting the evidence. It deals with facts of the world today. If you want, it expresses a statistical concern. "I see, taste, and hear something. What is it?" Such questions are answered

8. Psalm 8.

by shapes and numbers, texture, and other attributes, like hot and cold.

The question *why* asks for a cause, a reason, some necessary consequence to a prior condition of someone's choice. It looks for a more analytical response, including historical links or contributing factors to complex issues. *Why* also includes a hint of our sense that life is an unfinished business. You want to get to the bottom of it: there is room for doubt about the inevitability, the possible moral judgment, and a hope to avoid or to repeat, depending on what came together in the event that we wonder about. We transcend the moment, look for the context, and put the event or situation into a longer flow, stretching to include the "before" and "after."

Unlike a dog, who will bark at a stranger until he walks away, we wonder who the stranger might have been even after he is gone. Why did he come now? What was he looking for? Have we heard those steps before? Did we miss a friend, a UPS delivery, or in fact avoid a salesperson?

We long for an explanation to have a context and to tie up possible loose ends. We like to see the necessary links between events, an explanation for what is happening. We need to understand how it all stacks up. Then we can repeat it in our minds and understand why "it" worked out that way. We also discover possible mistakes that way and learn to avoid them the next time.

We have all made startling discoveries with this useful way of exploring reality and understanding the factors that lead up to a situation. So, since all babies are made between a man and a woman (that is the only way they come to be), therefore I also was conceived in this way. All people are put together to fall in love, to be attracted to the other, and to desire babies: most of the time that is the reason we come into the world. It is not a freak event, a random occurrence. There is a reasonable explanation that we are generally wanted when we are conceived. Only in this one particular fertility cycle could this particular person, this "I," possibly become actuality.

We expect explanations in all areas, because every avenue we pursue backwards leads us to either a rational, regularly occurring process that does not involve people, or to someone's more or less recent or historic choice to start a line of causations. Going back as far as we can, all events are either the result of a continuous process or of a single choice. When the cause is a single choice, it becomes evident that history is a record of things and events that did not really have to take place in *that* way. When a choice starts a chain of causes and effects, the choice was neither necessary nor inevitable. Necessary and inevitable is a choice-maker, a deliberate decision to proceed.

As shown above, the word *deliberate* indicates a freedom, a liberty at the start.

Yes, we are very familiar with a world of inevitable patterns in nature. Inevitability is a result of lawful behavior. Each natural phenomenon functions according to its kind. There are natural events that we experience as beneficial or as catastrophes. As a consequence we can know and take precautions and develop means to avoid or at least diminish destructive effects. We can anticipate, take medications without much fear, spend weeks in a submarine underwater, and survive, or fly across a continent to then land at the right place. We trust our lives to medical knowledge, drive skillfully at great speed along roads and remain safe, and return to our laboratory experiments the following day without doubt that we can continue where we have left off the night before.

We can do all that because there is a fundamental regularity to the world we inhabit, a fundamental rationality and lawfulness, and a confident predictability to a well-reasoned and carefully constructed exercise.

The human mind reflects and matches that predictability, also, in another interesting area: in the construction of language. Grammar and syntax, the definition of terms, words, and concepts, the construction of a sentence reflect the orderly shape of the outside world, about which conversation becomes then possible, from scientific essays to novels and poetry. Because there are no final surprises in the material world, no truly random and disconnected bits and pieces that, if they did exist, would require an equally random description impossible to understand, we can use the same kind of grammar to describe reality that we use to construct a language, in order to be able to talk about reality. There is a common basic grammar to the human mind, to communication between us, and to the world around us.

However, after saying all this on the side of rationality and order, we do not have the full picture. There remain painful disappointments, contradictions, deceptions, and really bad choices. That is also part of history. Early in life we have all encountered them in less than perfect parents, unfair teachers, broken friendships, and, later, corruptible judges and political propaganda. We know, or at least hear of wars, famine, corrupt officials, and bad government. In each case, a set of choices scratched or destroyed the hoped-for picture of consistently moral behavior. Even many natural catastrophes are the effect of prior human choices. The Roman practice of deforestation left much of Spain and Southern Italy with little and infertile topsoil. High numbers of casualties from the effects of earthquakes are often linked to corrupt builders and careless supervision. Personal choices of damaged people intersect with other people's lives in ways that are not deserved or expected.

A person's disregard for truth, honesty, known facts, and earlier commitments or accountability to law, whether those governing natural phenomena or defining an orderly community, is an original decision to redefine in his or her mind what should happen on a whim, from immoral motives or just because he or she has the power to do so. The results are painful and at times lethal. Pain, suffering, and scarred souls and minds can result from what people choose. While they express their humanity, their freedom to create, that freedom causes damage and destroys relationships.

Already nature is not always a comfortable or benevolent environment. Many parts of the earth's surface make life extremely unstable and untidy. Even our best insight does not remove tensions on the earth's surfaces, imbalances in natural resources and the food chain, or weather patterns inimical to life. Earthquakes, tsunamis, drought, and poison ivy are what human beings attempt to keep under control or far away. Their regular painful or lethal effects can be studied and, in some measure, acted against. But suffering from human failure originates in totally unnecessary personal choices, not a natural program.

It is in the nature of things and animals to function according to their template. It is in the nature of human beings, real personalities able to create, to act, for the most part, on the basis of choices. Nature has a program of closed reactions, while human beings act on the basis of chosen priorities, of evaluations they have embraced.

Fundamental elements of freedom in connection with human existence are evident in many other areas as well. The reality of language illustrates this, as language consists of arbitrarily chosen yet agreed-upon symbols of meaning for distinct objects and concepts, for relations and coordinates of experiences. Similar freedom is also presupposed when laws separate good from evil and guilt from innocence, praise from blame. It is experienced in the self-consciousness and first-person awareness of Descartes's "I think therefore I am." That freedom exists outside the realm of necessities. Choices are made there, which always create a history, but not a necessary or inevitable one.

The Bible gives mandates, commands, and judgments to encourage moral/cultural initiatives and choices. Outside its reach most people find such significance uncomfortable and even inconceivable. They submit instead to nature and history as a seamless, colorful band of necessary "normal" events, which become the "norms" of human inevitable existence.

This brings us to our next observation that in the absence of biblical insights nature is embraced as the standard for culture.

Chapter 2

The Reflection of Nature in Cultures

Human beings have always lived at the intersection of two significant influences. First, there is the natural world, which functions according to laws, regular patterns, and repeatable phenomena. Second, there are people, whose behavior is unpredictable, at times spontaneous, arbitrary, and willful, with at times great benefits for others, and then again great burdens. (I deliberately do not address the added reality of spiritual personages: the work of God or angels as well as the work of some demonic principalities. They fall under the reality of personal choices and their effects). Persons largely act by choice and with some intent, rather than by an inborn template; from learned or acquired behavior, rather than from instinct.

Undoubtedly persons do influence other persons by their chosen ways and their conversation, and in other ways do have an effect on others. Such an effect can be constraining or enlivening. We affect each other by scolding or by praise. But, in any case, it is centrally important to recognize and deal with the fundamental freedom of people to make choices.

Everyone seems to assume and claim such freedom. For that reason people have and impose commands, laws, or other social arrangements to prescribe limits to wrongdoing and to remind all of the content of such obligations as "love your neighbor as yourself" and "do not do such evils as commit adultery, invent multiple gods, violate property, bear false witness, murder, envy, or treat a person like a machine without a day off for rest." Such behaviors and their consequences are laid down in a norm and, with it, either encouraged or rejected, because it is possible behavior among people. Behaviors can be learned and practiced, for they are never instinctual or plain unavoidable.

We all find reasons to blame or praise others and hold them accountable or worthy.

Teaching norms for normal behavior assumes that it is not necessarily normal to follow them. Defining such rules also reveals that we as human beings expect to be able to control events in history by moral and intellectual opprobrium. Social and moral rules assume the existence of all kinds of personal actors as authors of the multiple and often contradictory and painful circumstances of life. Such rules are imposed on people by agreement from outside them. They exist to make a distinction between what is natural and what should be cultural.

The Bible certainly makes that clear distinction between nature's laws and man's cultural obligations. Things in nature are made first with form and in patterns, including a garden in Eden. That is nature functioning naturally. Adam and Eve were placed into it as people with mandates to act, to define and impose cultural choices. The sun, the moon, and the animals and plants were placed under man's dominion as much as his own personality. Man and woman received mandates to change what they found, to name what was unknown and nameless, and to create a larger world than what God had made.

According to Genesis, God did not intend creation to remain always the same, as if it were a museum piece: preserved, protected, and admired. He expected man and woman to figure out how they could depend on each other and become one, to create loving relations, and to choose to have more people on the earth than God had originally made. God expected, even mandated that they act, shape, create, and, with their minds and hands, alter what God had made to be used, subdued, and dominated.

It seems likely that when the human being was exiled from the garden and lost the immediate presence of God he had there, he soon began to make nature his home, his origin, and his closest neighbor. That is characteristic of many pagan cultures, so called from the Latin word *pagus* meaning "area, realm, grove in nature." Instead of walking with God as before (still possible by means of verbal instruction, a text, prophetic clarifications[1]), Man began to hug the trees and take his cues for life from silent nature, from the life modeled in animals under a closed firmament, as later described in Plato's dialogue *Timaeus* and Aristotle's *Nicomachean Ethics*.

That field of vision, limited to what exists under a closed heaven, explains the instinctual program of animals and the mechanical program of things. It contains a realm of dreaded circumstances as a result of the fall of Adam and Eve in normal human experience. Until the biblical view of reality demystified the natural world, all occurrences in

---

1. Boorstin, *Seekers*, 7. "Through the prophets God governed his people."

nature were seen to be acts of personalities, spirits, gods, demons, and occult forces.

I suggested just now that this way of seeing is essentially pagan. We find it in Greek thought and in many religions and cultures around the world. It projects on the world of trees, mountains, and the sea around them the capabilities we observe in human beings to act and to produce results. Since the man and the woman produce results and consequences by their surprising choices, similar personal activists, either gods or spirits, must move things by equally surprising choices from behind the curtain, from the unseen world into the seen world. All events among and above natural settings were thought to be caused by someone bigger than people, but functioning much like them. Such personages were imagined to be hidden, devious, or openly brutal, Man, spirits, or God. All reality was accepted to be inhabited by conscious personages, souls, spirits, or anima, summed up under the term *animism*. There was little understanding that much in nature simply functions "according to its kind," following a determined program.

Since personages were known to make choices, and since there was little knowledge of the nature of a fallen creation, all experiences of a difficult or tragic life also came one's way by someone's choice. Gods and fates were the initiators of one's cruel destiny, the malefactors of your circumstances.

An animist cultural context will personalize everything. Every stone and tree, ever brook and pond, every conquest or illness is the manifestation of someone's action. Your relation to the world around you is personal: you honor, fear, talk with and to, bring food and make amends, apologize and pray with the expectation and hope that this someone will act favorably, assuage his or her anger, and turn away from you towards your neighbor instead. You pay attention to this hidden personage, animus, or anima from fear!!

In that view of the world, water does not come forth in a spring or source; it is a spirit that spits forth the liquid. Thunder is the sound of gods bowling again. Floods are the rage of Neptune of the seas. An infection is sign of the ill will of a neglected deity. The shaman, priest, or medicine man will claim to have access to the life behind the curtain that separates the visible from the invisible world. He will tell you what is to be done to bring about again that fragile equilibrium that your neglect has unbalanced. Like weights of lead added here and there on the rim of a wheel to balance it, his work will make life run smoothly again. Until you once again hit against a curve in history!

Homer's great epic stories of the *Iliad* and the *Odyssey* bring to life for us the multiple divinities and their helpers during the years long before later philosophers attempted to bring order to this lively, though very confusing bunch of characters. No god had one single character. There was no certainty of commitment of each god to his protégé. Gods, men, and women would change their minds and loyalties as often as the wind turned in the sails of the ships anchored before Troy.

Animism and similar superstitions are not limited to times past, though Judaism and Christianity (and their descendent prodigal son of secularism) have largely removed them from our daily experience. Yet we still have statues of river gods in Europe, which now have a Saint's head and name as a sign of a past Roman Catholic dominance. Many today still knock on wood (representing the Cross of Christ) to not be punished for their pleasure or any good thing by an "evil eye." In the Buryatia Republic of Russia, people will throw money along the road or over the bridge for safe travel in cars with unfit brakes. They will sprinkle vodka into the wind and break up cigarettes along the road in the hope of sharing these pleasures with spirits and thus being kept safe and immune to lung cancer.

The Nobel-Prize-winning author V. S. Naipaul, in his latest book "The Mask of Africa," describes some observations about religions in Africa. In Gabon the dense forest is home to all the evils that threaten human life. Sickness, wild animals, spirits have their home there and make life for people so miserable and insecure. There is no concept of a "good life." Even the trees must be asked before they are felled. All of life, including that of the jungle, is energy, from it one feeds and to it the body returns at death. To survive, one kills and eats body parts, preferably from albinos for the energy they contain, and sacrifices human organs. The world is organic, made up of flowers and fauna, the life in the jungle. It is evident that god has no time for human beings, who live in constant fear, including the fear of women, who are considered witches, because they give birth to yet more human beings and thereby prolong and multiply the pain of existence.

For many centuries people everywhere have attempted to explain the uncertainty of human willful actions and the ignorance about nature's laws with similar views and customs. Common is the assumption that there is a powerful personal being behind everything, to be both welcomed and feared. Believers adhere to that explanation; the process "works," whatever is meant with that, by any, not only our standards. They turn their unexamined experiences into a worldview and accept this explanation all the way to the end, regardless of the cost to life and thought, to body and mind: that, also, whatsoever it may be, is assumed to be the working of fate, the will of God or Allah or, in our scientific orientation, the dominance of genetic determinants.

For in the end these views assume that everything "was somehow meant to be."

TYRANNICAL CONTROL VERSUS A TRINITY OF COMPASSION

But such a bewildering collection of unpredictable, amoral, and immoral personages of spirits and gods is not reliable. Many gods lack a common intentionality and present no harmonious moral fabric. Multiple roots of power breed anarchy, and the human mind longs for order, cohesion, and resolution. Something else had to be found that would give more stability, fewer seemingly random events. The alternative was something like a super-divinity, a God behind gods or some other form of encompassing totalitarian authority. A unifying answer would explain all the various events and would give resolution to disparate interpretations: a unifying principle to tie all ends together, to present a closed package of reality.

The striving for a unity is clearly urgent in a world threatened by chaos. Social beings long for conversation, not cacophony. Without unity, even a unity of terms and language, there is no rest, no foundation, and no common meaning. It is well known that Mohammed made the effort to unite various tribal deities under one god, Allah. The disparate divinities and idols among Bedouin tribes encouraged rivalries. Mohammed recognized that strength against the expanding Byzantine Christianity in the north and Ethiopian Coptic Christianity along the trade route to India in the south could only come through unity.

In other societies, the call for a central government often becomes strongest when chaos threatens civility. Israel was to remember at all times that, "Behold o Israel, the Lord your God is one." That oneness affirms a fundamental ordered existence, a unity of authority and truth, as well as the uniqueness to the God of the Bible. The Lord God is singularly God.

However, only this personal-infinite and infinite-personal God of the Bible explains fully our humanity, our diverse personhood in his image. Only the character of this God lays the foundation for love and grace from inside his own character, rather than establishing arbitrary power and authoritarian rule. Knowing this God will allow people to find order short of tyranny, and freedom short of anarchy.

For, to love God and his commands with all our heart, mind, and soul, and our neighbor as ourselves, is the response to a single God in the high order of Trinity. Love, like grace, is part of his Being, and not an occasional choice. They are among the attributes of God, not expressions of an occasional will of God. This removes the danger of a divine tyranny from God, which would otherwise make the people so afraid that they would not argue with God. This particular anchor in a biblical unity never produced the totalitarian relationship we find in other places when all is blindly gathered under authority.

When God is understood to be infinite in his attributes, but not in the extension of his being, we understand that God is not everything, like Greek fates or Marxist movements of history. God is not the cosmos. The Bible does not start with a unity of Being, an Infinity, but with One God in substance and three eternal persons. Unity and diversity are at the start of any consideration of the biblical view of reality, history, and our place as human beings in that history.

In other words, the Bible emphasizes as much the sole sovereignty of God as the distinct uniqueness of each person in the Trinity. The Father is not the Son. They decided, together with the Spirit, to create a real world of increasing distinctions. Distinction is the mark of reality as much as its harmony, rationality, logic, and consistency. The Bible does not talk about everything being finally *one*. God is, but he created a real world outside himself, vis-à-vis, instead of being an extension of God.

The need to recognize, follow, and treasure distinctions is taught through the whole Bible. On its foundation we find the structure of moral judgments, intellectual rigor, and a sequential view of distinct historical events. Distinctions in all manner of reality keep things separate, ideas clear, and responsibility defined.

Distinctions are real in the realms of being and in the consideration of morals. God's ideas of history can be thwarted by new choices, which include also contrary choices on the part of the creature. Man, male and female, is free to create and thereby to bring about things that give

God pleasure and possibly also pain, grief, or additional tasks. Consequently new things can always occur, moral wrong can be committed and justice established. God is not the only player on the stage of history or in nature. Instead, there is in fact a complex interaction of God and the personages he made with real significance. They affect history by their choices, for better or for worse.

History is then not just what had to happen under the mantle of sovereign decrees and the perfect will of God, fate, or natural powers. The Bible does not describe a closed system of pushes and shoves. It does not speak of a sovereign will that cannot possibly be thwarted or disturbed. The Oneness of Eastern religions, the will of Allah in Islam, the Inevitability of scientific progress in Hegelian Marxism, the rule by fate or spirit, even scientific rationalism are each different from what the Bible tells us. There is no finally controlled situation. Each day inherits the past and receives enrichment or impoverishment through the will of the Creator and that of personal creatures. That, but not all the particular choices, is what the God of the Bible decreed.

The human being can defy God, but not step outside his universe. He can make God's work ugly, but he cannot keep God from getting back to work to heal things. He can complicate history, but not leave it to random events and occurrences, or lock the door to later life-changing initiatives. We do not ever live in a closed system from here on forward. A soccer game will always end with a goal, either in the course of the game or by penalty shots in overtime. A balloon or a kite is widely tossed about by the wind, but will always be anchored to the string that holds it.

GOD AND MAN: INTERVENTIONIST TEAM

When Adam and Eve sinned, God the Lord went back to work. He had rested on the seventh day from all his labor, because it was accomplished and could now be fully enjoyed. But with the Fall of Man something else had to be done by God to repair what sin had damaged and put under death. The Lamb of God, known by God "from before the foundation of the world," was God's way to deal with guilt and death. Now it had to be prepared and eventually slain. Having invested so much pleasure, such care for detail, such beauty in the garden, such perfection in creating the human being, God was determined not to abandon his investment in created personages.

So he ran after Adam, called him out of his hiding place among the bushes, addressed his shame and guilt, and set to work himself for his creation, which was now marked in all parts by the dust of death. (The often eight-sided baptismal fountain in churches, or the octagonal towers you see, are a symbolic representation of what God accomplished on the eighth day of creation. That was the day when Christ, the Messiah, rose from the dead to demonstrate that God had conquered sin, guilt, and death itself!)

But none of that was necessary. There was nothing automatic about Adam and Eve's sin, nothing prescribed to be followed. No plan to be fulfilled, no eternal counsel set in heaven that everything had to happen the way it did. And of course in a sense there was also no necessity for God to step into work again, except by choice to love and to be faithful to his own commitment and character.

For that reason, we speak of a flow to history. We look back from our vantage point at any time and see why things happened. We find answers to our questions. We investigate crimes, we remember who invented what, and we recognize the corruption and failures or successes of this or that person. Such links, from hindsight, demonstrate to us that we do live in a world of consequential order, of connections, of reasons for events. It is not at all a random world of disconnected bits and pieces, of isolated events. There is significance in the smallest detail. We find a reason behind all things. Our minds require a set of connecting links as much as we seek to understand any sentence in a document from the reasonable use of words and grammar. We also find that the real world around us functions in similar patterns of reasonable relations, of fitting joints. Water always runs downhill. Something lost or misplaced can only be in one place and not two. When I have carefully looked for it in the top drawer of my dresser, I do not have to look there again. (Unless of course I forgot what I was looking for, which easily happens to me.)

Past superstitions have happily been replaced by reasoned insight gained from prior experiences, analysis, and observations, where the way our minds see and make links or connections at all times brings relief in the form of confident certainties.

But it would be a mistake to conclude from such neat links in the material and impersonal world that there is inevitability also about the choices a person made previously. We can make causal links backwards to such choices along the path of the effects they had. With every decision in the past to act come necessary effects in time towards our point of interest. By making a choice, one orchestrates the consequences. The link between event and what follows can be known, as history has moved on from choice to consequence. There is no other way a rational universe functions. We count on it every day of our lives.

INDIVIDUALS MATTER MORE

Many clear human choices alter the course of events in most of the dramatic changes in known history. Let me give some illustrations. You may remember how the Battle of Hastings in 1066 was won by the Norman Duke William II when an arrow penetrated the eye of King Harold II. William became the "Conqueror" and imposed French as the spoken language for the next three hundred years at court and among the intellectuals under the Kings of England. The roots of many Romance components of the English language are found in this historic change made by a personal choice. No longer does English only have words from the language of the barnyard. French brought the language of the court. It separated the table of the nobility from the stable of the common person. The French word *boeuf* became the English *beef*, a courtly alternative to the word *cow* from its Saxon root and German word *Kuh*. To the relational importance of *freedom*, from the Germanic root *Freiheit*, was added the rational/intellectual concept of liberty from *libertas* in Latin.

Similarly significant, but closer to our own time of history, were the choices not to advance with the destruction of the towns of Heidelberg and Rothenburg in Germany. Unlike most other cities at the end of World War II, these two remained largely intact, because in each case the mayor or some other high official chose to hand the town over to the approaching allied armies. In the case of Rothenburg, the request for such a hand-over came from the American commander, whose mother had told him of the beauty and wholeness of the town's medieval architecture and composition. He decided to ask for surrender rather than military conquest from a desire to see for himself the walled treasure lying in front of his troops, about which his mother had talked to him in such vividly descriptive terms.

Contrast this set of choices with those Pharaoh made in the Bible. When the announced plague of hail (Exodus 9:13–26) contains a promise of protection for those animals and people that are brought in from the fields and open spaces to be sheltered in stables and homes (19–21), some Egyptians chose to obey and saved their livestock and themselves. Others chose to disregard the warning. And when the hail stopped, because Moses prayed, Pharaoh again chose to break his earlier promise to let the people go.

In recent history, we can consider the tremendously weighty significance of Niels Bohr's decision not to go to the Allied side in World War II, with all his knowledge about nuclear fission, until they had arranged for him to be lifted out of Sweden, where he had fled earlier on from his beloved Denmark, now occupied by Nazi forces and their administration. Instead he stayed and argued with the King of Sweden, whom he finally convinced to accept as refugees from Nazi persecution what turned out to be most of the Jewish population of his native Denmark. As the Nazis set in motion the first round-up, many Danish citizens at first hid Jews in all sorts of hiding places until they were able to then ferry 90 percent of them across the Oresund to Sweden in more than 700 nightly trips.

An earlier, similarly vivid illustration for the singularly weighty choices of one person altering the flow of history is found in the events related about Ambrose, archbishop of Milan in the fourth century. He descended from a noble Roman family in Gaul. His father had been a Praetorian Prefect, and he himself had been governor before being called to the ecclesiastical office. In the conflict with the Western Roman Emperor, who was theologically an Arian and not true to the Trinitarian teaching of the church, he refused the Empress Justina and her entourage—including her second husband Valentinian, canopy, and all—access to the Basilica, when she came to celebrate Easter there in public devotion.

Follow these significant details of the events from Gibbon's account:

> "(Ambrose) was followed, without his consent, by an innumerable crowd, (which) pressed with impetuous zeal against the gates of the palace; and the affrighted ministers of Valentinian, instead of pronouncing a sentence of exile on the archbishop of Milan, humbly requested that he would interpose his authority to protect the person of the emperor and to restore the tranquility of the capital. The city was agitated by the irregular convulsions of tumult and fanaticism. The officers of the household were directed to prepare . . . the new Basilica, for the immediate reception of the emperor and his mother. The splendid canopy and hangings of the royal seat

were arranged in the customary manner; but it was found necessary to defend them by a strong guard from the insults of the populace. The Arian ecclesiastics, who ventured to show themselves in the streets, were exposed to the most imminent danger of their lives; and Ambrose enjoyed the merit and reputation of rescuing his personal enemies from the hands of the enraged multitude.

"But while he labored to restrain the effects of their zeal, the . . . vehemence of his sermons continually inflamed the angry and seditious temper of the people of Milan". Arianism "was compared to the most-cruel persecutions which Christianity had endured under the reign of Paganism. The measures of the court served only to expose the magnitude of the evil. . . . The ministers of Valentinian imprudently confessed that the most respectable part of the citizens of Milan was attached to the cause of their archbishop.

"He (Ambrose) was again solicited to restore peace to his country, by timely compliance with the will of his sovereign. The reply of Ambrose was couched in the most humble and respectful terms, which might, however, be interpreted as a serious declaration of civil war. 'His life and fortune were in the hands of the emperor; but he would never betray the church of Christ, or degrade the dignity of the Episcopal character. In such a cause he was prepared to suffer whatever the malice of the daemon could inflict; and he only wished to die in the presence of his faithful flock, and at the foot of the altar; he had not contributed to excite, but it was in the power of

God alone to appease, the rage of the people: he deprecated the scenes of blood and confusion which were likely to ensue; and it was his fervent prayer, that he might not survive to behold the ruin of a flourishing city, and perhaps the desolation of all Italy."[2] The obstinate bigotry of Justina would have endangered the empire of her son Theodosius, if, in this contest with the church and people of Milan, she could have depended on the active obedience of the troops of the palace. A large body of Goths had marched to occupy the Basilica, which was the object of the dispute: and it might be expected from the Arian principles, and barbarous manners, of these foreign mercenaries, that they would not entertain any scruples in the execution of the most sanguinary orders. They were encountered, on the sacred threshold, by the archbishop, who, thundering against them a sentence of excommunication, asked them, in the tone of a father and a master, whether it was to invade the house of God that they had implored the hospitable protection of the republic. The suspense of the Barbarians allowed some hours for a more effectual negotiation; and the empress was persuaded, by the advice of her wisest counselors, to leave the Catholics in possession of all the churches of Milan; and to dissemble, till a more convenient season, her intentions of revenge. The mother of the populace of Milan became enraged over the provocation by the Imperial power to claim also the building of the Church."[3]

2. Footnoted in Gibbon, but without indication of its origin
3. Gibbon, *Decline and Fall*, volume 3, chapter XXVII (Civil

On a personal note, my father recognized without much effort the significance of the Potsdam Conference in the summer of 1945. It ended on the decision to evict all populations of German origin from all of Eastern Europe. Father understood that this would lead to great social chaos in a war-torn Western Europe. Stalin would achieve what he intended. Like a ripe apple falls from the tree, the rest of Europe beyond the reach of the Soviet army would also fall into the hands of Stalin's Soviet Communism. Potsdam decreed that millions of additional people would swell an already confused and impoverished population further west. A social catastrophe would ensue.

Father saw the need to alert the occupying powers, specifically the U.S., and went from one commanding officer to the next, explaining the historic situation and requesting material help. Housing, tools, reconstruction credits, schools, and markets had to be provided to receive a freight train load of expellees each week. That choice had to be made, or Stalin would pick the fallen fruit. I remember that Captain Stentson, commander in my hometown, recognizing what burden Stalin's plans had imposed, carried out countermeasures. Refugees were cared for as much as possible, and Stalin's forces were stopped at what later became the Iron Curtain. Warsaw, Budapest, and Prague were swallowed by the Soviet army, but Berlin, Vienna, Athens, and capitals further west were spared by real choices on the part of many individuals.

Wars, Reign of Theodius, part 1) is accessible at http://www.gutenberg.org/dirs/2/5/7/1/25717/25717-h/files/733/733-h/gib3-27.htm#2HCH0003

Choices contribute to the direction in the flow of history. By individual choices events are created and shaped, and others are avoided. There is neither a random set of occurrences nor a closed program of necessities that make up what we know and experience as history. The kingpin of history is each person's significance, the power to decide and to own results, both with pride and with shame.

Chapter 3

The Weight of Significance

Philosophers may argue whether there is such a thing as a cause, i.e., whether an event causes another. A cause has never been seen as a separate thing. But what everyone admits is that when one billiard ball knocks against another the second one will start to move, and the first will be redirected. We commonly call this effect on the second as caused by the first, a kind of transference of motion, of energy, which is related to object and motion permanence.

In our common world we see that choices always have consequences somewhere, sooner or later. We cannot have our cake after we have already eaten it. There cannot be an omelet without breaking the eggs first. Whoever falsely cries "wolf" is hard to believe the next time. A stone thrown into a pool of water creates ripples across its surface. All these illustrations reflect the fact that past actions have present consequences. Something happens as a consequence of an earlier event or a choice.

Even the choice of God to work a miracle has measurable consequences, no less than that God's choice to create a real world way back then means that now there is a world. Those 5000 people fed by Jesus on the mountain came back the next day for more, because they had been fed. The blind could now see, the leper could leap about.

But we cannot observe links into a real future until someone becomes a cause—makes a choice and acts. Until a choice is made we face an open field ahead of us: where we choose to walk, whether we throw stones or simply set up our tools and paint from the water's edge. Only after the results become evident can we figure things out backwards from evidence to cause. In front is real freedom; behind is the choice, made with inevitable consequences. Then, we had alternatives, but now, the outcome is definite. What in time lies before or earlier determined the later outcome. But, in front, only a person determines what will happen. That is the nature of real significance: the ability to alter the course of history forward or from then on out. The field ahead is open. We choose an activity, which is bound to its consequences. We ate, and now it is time to pay up.

What I describe here is genuine sovereignty, given to each person within the limits of prior conditions and inherited historical and personal settings. Looking back, we are bound by what went before. Looking ahead, none of us is a total prisoner of circumstance. Even if someone were to tie down our bodies, we would be free in our thoughts, as Heine said at a time of increasing government censure in the nineteenth century. In our minds, we judge the present and imagine alternatives.

The classical Roman statesman of the fourth century, Boethius, a highly educated Christian, also sought freedom. He imagined a lady, Philosophy, to speak to him with words of comfort in the agony of his unjustified incarceration. She drew on ideas from Greek philosophy to disregard his experiences in real but temporary misery, urging him to focus his mind on a permanent ideal elsewhere. She told him something that in a secular version would suggest, "In the greater scheme of things, what you go through is nothing." As a Christian he resolved to not really object to injustice, as all experiences are part of a larger program. In the end, he was told, even the pain and injustice would serve him well. Heine did not go the route of Greek idealism but stayed on the hard surface of real wrong.

Basically Boethius assumes that reality is an illusion, that life in time and space is not really real, that historic choices for good and ill have no real consequences after all. This view has often crept into Christian thought, where people have adopted Greek philosophic reflection and abandoned biblical teaching. For the Bible insists on the significance of each event, each person, and each choice as playing a part in the greater scheme of things. Because of all the choices by people with historic results, God interferes, confronts, and will judge. Because of the many bad choices of sovereign persons, Christ came to work redemption, i.e., to undo both guilt and death. In the Bible, the talk is not about some outside ultimate purpose that absorbs all details or minimizes their importance. Quite to the contrary, because of the weight of the details, God is engaged to repel sin, to conquer death, and to bring in his kingdom. The God of the Bible wrestles against evil, strives against sin and promises to make things right.

Heine's view is, as a Jewish perspective, much closer to the biblical one.

When I use the term *sovereignty* in this context, I want to stress that the nature of choice is the unconditioned and original behavior of an open mind. In a choice, a person clarifies intentions, chooses actions, controls reactions, and is a self, sovereign in that small, yet so very significant moment and place. The field mentioned above will give you pleasure for your picnic, but only if you or someone else did not previously cover it with stones or trash. If you want to paint the field, you may want to wait before spreading out your picnic. It is still an undisturbed field, but not for long. The grass will be trampled down, even after you have picked up all your wrappings, plastic cups, and paper tissues. Not to mention what the dog may have left behind!

But at the moment of making a choice, the situation is very specific. Ahead all is open; behind, or afterwards, much is limited. The choice exists within the limits of the past, but each new moment in time and location in space has its own openness. What will you choose to do now, here?

Alternatively, if the past sets the parameters for all your moves, there is nothing significant about yourself or this time and place. Any already determined program, divine or natural, fated or due to scientific rationality, robs the person of any true significance. There is no action, only reaction. No choice, only a necessary move.

Without significance, there is no reason to attach praise or blame to a person's choice. Yet that certainly does not correspond to the view of the world we have, express, and practice.

This becomes evident when you observe that all human languages always contain words of praise and accusation, admiration and critique. Language uses prescriptive as well as descriptive vocabulary, which would be unfitting and mostly meaningless in an already determined world.

Our association of events, inventions, and things with individual people would be a cynical joke if they had nothing significant to do with them.

What lifted our cultural context out of the widely held views of fate, gods, science, and other forms of determinism was the instruction about human significance found in the Bible, in Jewish and Christian thought, through the centuries and the cultures that that thought brought about.

The Bible's focus is on God's relation to individual people in real history. It contains few general stories, but much about people with names and their choices in real life. History is not a ribbon of events, but a fabric woven by individuals who choose the threads, the colors, as it were, the buttons, the pattern, and all the rest. We read how that garment is made over time by tailors and seamstresses who make up the human race. We recognize a past time and how that shapes a future. It is the account of God creating Adam and Eve, making an eternal promise to Abraham and his descendants, and placing the Son of God on the throne of David. People in the Bible have names and distinct personalities. They are addressed by prophets, marry a wife, and beget numerous children with separate names. The lists with names of good and bad kings, true and false prophets, faithful and unfaithful priests transmit how significant individuals affect the world around them, the generations after them, and God's relationship to all people. Individuals, not mankind or an anonymous people group, are the main actors on the stage of history.

GOD AMONG MESSY PEOPLE

Against the history of their unpredictable choices stands the faithful continuity of God's relation with the children of Abraham. They are willful, stubborn, obstinate, foolish, and often change their mind. They forget, they argue, and they repent. Over against such contradictory behavior, God "changes his mind" only in response to a foolish, unfaithful, and finally irrational choice of a human being. In each case this "change of mind" is but the changed moral content of God's unchanging character in relationship to people and situations.

The situation changes, for instance, when Moses intercedes for the people,[1] and consequently God has a changed response to it. God chooses at all times to love and favor his creatures. Man at times chooses to play god and to assume he can define reality in his own image, create laws that favor him over others, and interpret social responsibility in a selfish manner. Such decisions create a very untidy world, the one we are also familiar with through daily exposure. It is a world with loose ends, unresolved, with real injustice and horrible pain.

It is thoughtless and no help to suggest that such a world and the choices that lead to it is what God ordained in some mysterious way, or that it is not so bad after all because it all could be much worse. At all times, the Bible affirms the genuine sovereignty of free decision by the creature, which can cause God's plans to be thwarted. Is it not for that reason that God went back to work after the fall of Adam and on the eighth day raised Christ from the dead? God is at work

1. Exod 33, 34.

to correct, to redeem, to inform, to encourage in a situation of our alienation from God, due to choices made and their consequences, inherited by later generations. The sins of the fathers fall on many generations. God's work is a real effort with a certain outcome. But it is a continuing effort—we could say labor-intensive—until it is accomplished.

I am always surprised how many people want to avoid such a conclusion already in the present. They want to declare everything resolved, tidy, and in place under God at all times. But one cannot have it both ways: to notice genuine wrong and at the same time not be too troubled by it. And yet that is what happens when people hold to a divinely appointed, decreed plan both of and from God's sovereignty, whereby nothing is ever not what it was meant to be and everything happens because of necessity for God's purposes, and yet at one and the same time they affirm genuine and free human action. They embrace comfortably a belief that in fact removes the untidiness and tragedy of real wrong by accepting everything as already planned, willed, and purposed. For them nothing is out of place at any time. They want this to be the best of all possible worlds, because nothing is askew. But they also want to be able to object to illness, crime, bad government, and the disturbing behavior of their children (or their parents: it depends on who is talking).

I have suggested previously in my book *The Innocence of God*[2] how that view results in either fatalism or in arrogance: either nothing should be done about a fallen world, or everything I can get away with must be part of God's perfect plan.

2. *The Innocence of God* (Colorado Springs, Authentic/STL, 2007).

That is, however, not the picture the Bible gives. For, the God of the Bible, knowing all things, including the end from the beginning and all the foolish choices we will make in a lifetime, does not will all things (permissively or otherwise), nor does he ever experience all things in some timeless and "eternal now."[3] He does not reveal his will by means of the events of history, the record of what took place. Instead he speaks in language, sentences, in his Word, to enable us to critique and judge what happens.

The text is also the record of what he in his character had in mind. Stuff happens: kings are chosen, priests function, and Apostles preach; but whether it expresses the will and mind of God is not decided merely on the basis of any of these events alone. Rather, events, including Peter's return to legalistic Jewish prescriptions, are reprimanded or approved on the basis of the text, understood to be the Word of God. It is the set of glasses by which we see God's mind and character more accurately. It serves as a filter to keep out the most obvious impurities. We live by the Word, not by bread alone!

The Word became flesh and dwelt among us.[4] Prophets spoke as they were borne by the Holy Spirit.[5] Jesus gives a precise reflection of the Father.[6] His teaching, life, and interaction with the people of his time help us understand who God is.

---

3. I suggest this idea among Christians to reflect Greek philosophic thought; it is not a biblical idea. The distinction between eternal foreknowledge and sequential experience makes all the difference, as I lay it out in *The Innocence of God*.

4. John 1.

5. 2 Pet 1:19–21.

6. Heb 1:3.

GOD'S WILL AT ODDS WITH HISTORY

God's mind and will do not at all times coincide with the flow of history. In contrast to the suggestion that the will of God is being carried out already in all things in history, the Bible gives us multiple illustrations that things and events did not have to occur. We need to affirm genuine and free human actions that can follow God's directions or can oppose them.

There is then no necessity or compulsion for any event, most of the time, merely as a result of God's interaction with people. The people with real names in the Bible are not automata or pawns in the hands of God. They are addressed on the level of their minds, by language and concepts, by the power of God's Spirit, to say or do things. They had the choice to follow or to disregard and forget. God speaks, but also pleads and laments, praises and accuses, laughs and weeps, as he engages with an untidy world of human beings in a very differentiating manner.

Without such a real choice for people made in the image of God, there would be no praise for faithfulness and no condemnation of sin, no place to admire or to grieve. If every event or human action was already programmed, nothing could have been different from the way it all happened.

All history would be necessary and inevitable. That view is taught in scientific materialism and practiced in what we know as Marxism. It is also the view held in Islam, African tribal religions, scientific naturalism. Daniel Boorstin describes it as "a belief that history is governed by its own iron rules, and that man is not free to shape his own experience."[7] It is a form of religious or secular reduction-

---

7. Boorstin, *Seekers*, 54.

ism. But that view is not found in the Bible, neither does it correspond to our observation of living history, which presents us with many more chaotic situations.

After a number of years under the rule of prophets and judges, the people Israel desired to have a king, in fact to become like other nations, replacing God as their sovereign with the sovereignty of human kings. There is a parallel here to the hunger for immediate certainty and the comfort of being under someone's control when many Christians have drawn upon divine determinism as a presupposition for understanding history. With great ease, though often unaware, they have wandered, philosophically, from Jerusalem to Athens, from Jehovah to Zeus, from Moses to Plato.

With that presupposition, God, man, and history would all become parts of the same gigantic program of necessities. Jewish and Christian teaching from the Scriptures alone had liberated us from such a view of reducing everything to impersonal necessities, to all-embracing providence, and natural selection. With this alternative view to the Bible's, we are all bound in the determined effects of divine purposes and thereby turn God into nothing different or better than another Greek god, only this time more powerful.

THE END IS SURE, THE WAY UNCERTAIN

According to the biblical record, history could have gone in many other directions without making God less sovereign or turning reality into a random series of events. There is a form to the universe, but also a reality of freedoms. There is an inherited context passed on, but also an element of genuine, unpredictable novelty in each person and each new situation.

In Genesis, we read that Adam and Eve were uniquely formed from the dust by God, who breathed in them the breath of life, so that they became living souls. Everything else came out of the dust, the stuff that God had made at the beginning. There was something distinct about human beings, which was their personhood, their being in the image of the creator. They had minds, imagination, and choice. God placed them into a created world and gave them work to do that would change, vary, and increase what was there before. They would choose their relationship, which God did not prescribe, model, or spell out. They would give names to animals and have other forms of dominion over creation and themselves. They would do good, love God and each other, and create beauty by choice, not by mechanisms.

By choice they would please God and obey the one command they had, which served as a tripwire to make love for God something more than a general state of existence. There was nothing wrong in the garden as described. The prohibition to eat from the tree was to give evidence of an external distinction between love and indifference to God, between attention and disregard, between reverence and revolt. It made clear the difference between living in God's world or a world of their imagination and making.

For probably many years, they knew nothing but what was good, in the company of God and one another. I am confident that what we have as the "Fall of Adam and Eve" was not their first choice ever, though many see it that way. They all too easily forget what we know from the account, that Adam and Eve rightly and lovingly chose each other, recognizing over time the wonder of true humanity and love, of dependence and satisfaction, of the help one was to the other in their union as they walked and talked with God.

When they then fell from God, they chose to consider in their minds an alternative, a wider possible world, to which Satan invited them with the promise that they "could be like God." They chose to turn from God and heard another word, a lie in fact, which had an appealing ring to it. Just like the fruit, beautiful and pleasant to look at, so also was the promise of a beautiful extension of their existence into god-like experience. It was deceptive, because there was no way that creatures could become infinite. They had a beginning; how could they become eternal like God?

But they fell for it with all the tragic consequences that surround us on all sides.

This is the first instance in which we see how history, human choices, did not have to take on the shape it has. Adam and Eve were in no way compelled, neither by character nor by circumstances nor from ignorance. They knew the consequence of disobedience, as God had told them that they would die by losing all they had: life, conversation, presence of God, and the original peaceable kingdom of the Garden of Eden. They were sent east of Eden, and all of us were born there in that condition, which they created by their choice.

God urged them not to go that way. He told them ahead of time what the consequences would be. He had made them perfect "in the image of God" and without flaws. There was no need for them to listen to the temptation, as they had everything for a continuously fulfilling and active life. There was no need to know both good and evil intimately in order for them to enjoy the knowledge and experience of good only.

There was no plan of God as a result of which Adam and Eve would or should fall. There was neither reward nor merit, no benefit from such actions. When Christians have read into the fall *ex post facto* some justification for its necessity, it is only an attempt to see a purpose, a necessity, the will of God, and other ways, to diminish real human significance. They can accomplish such theological gymnastics only by neglecting Scripture and in the end presenting a very different God from the one revealed through history in Scripture.

Several of the church fathers suggest that we ought to be thankful for the sin of Adam and Eve, since without it we would have never known God's grace in Christ. That makes little sense, as our first parents had the closest possible relation with the Trinity in the garden already. Justifying the horror of the fall in this way is parallel to so many Christians today who accept any horrible event as part of the perfect plan of God and therein find a justification for the event. A parent runs over his child with his car is said to reveal that God purposed a short life for the child?! A handicapped child is given to a family to teach them patience? Using such reasoning, nothing is ever out of place, wrong, or regrettable. It is a case of justifying the means to get to the desired end.

The desired end is peace of mind, but the way there involves cruelty to the child and to God, who all along makes every effort to disassociate himself from human sin and folly!

NO INHERITED GUILT OR FAULT

Adam and Eve are our ancestors, and by their choice they affect us all. None of us is quite normal, we are all damaged people. They were, however, neither our representatives, nor did they make us all guilty by their revolt. That is a non sequitur in both law and theology. Damage is a result of inheritance, while guilt is the result of individual wrong choices. Criminals are guilty only for themselves. Yet their actions affect all that live in their circle of influence after them. In that sense we are all children of Adam and Eve. We all suffer as a result of their actions, but are not guilty in or from them. Our life is not the same as it was meant to be, but we are not responsible for all of it. Each of us now lives in a broken world and is, like they, damaged in a state of imperfection and prone to sin. But responsible are we for it only in the measure of our subsequent guilty contribution to its mess.

God does not see us guilty merely because we are descendants from earlier generations in the human race. Paul describes it in this manner: "Therefore, just as sin entered the world through one man, and death through sin, in this way death came to all men, because all sinned."[8] Death, not guilt, is inherited. When it is the result of a free choice, sin produces guilt. However, sin as a state of inherited imperfections does not indicate a level of personal guilt.

The young man born blind[9] had a condition that is quite frequent in a fallen reality. His damaged sight resulted precisely not from his or his parents' guilt, but from a less

8. Rom 5:12.
9. John 9.

than perfect reality. Since he already had his problem, Jesus could show the work of God in him. God did not give him the blindness for a superior end, for to God the end does not justify the means!

In summary, there was no necessity for Adam's sin. He made a choice that affects all history afterwards, including the history of God's relation to his creation into our own days. God makes a choice to go back to work, as mentioned before. He knew he would and already had prepared "the lamb from before the foundation of the world." But this preparation was not the necessary cause for the choice of Adam and Eve's revolt.

PASSIONATE EFFORTS OF REDRESS

We find repeatedly that God has multiple plans and ways and choices to address, and eventually to fully remedy, all manner of effects from alternate original choices and the failures that follow human creativity.

In the fourth chapter of Genesis, we see that again: history, the record of events and choices, is not a list of necessary occurrences. No, Cain did not have to kill Abel. It could have gone another way, and all of subsequent history would have been affected differently.

We read that Cain's offering of the fruit of his work in the soil was not acceptable to God, while Abel's animal sacrifice was. The reason for that distinction is not arbitrary on the part of God. Nor are the chosen sacrifices on the part of the two children of Adam and Eve arbitrary. Instead of figuring out possible reasons for the original sacrifice and going back to its meaning in the Jewish perspective, Cain invented something to please God. That was rejected, because it did not contain the purpose of a sacrifice, but was something like a play. Cain refused to believe God, while Abel believed.[10]

The rejection made Cain angry. In fact, God warns Cain and holds out a different reaction to his offering "if you do what is right." And what is that? Abel brought an offering in line with the offering God had made when he killed an animal to cover up Adam and Eve's guilt and nakedness. It was a symbolic admission of guilt, repaired through the substitute death of an animal, in anticipation of the release from guilt and death through the sacrifice of the "true lamb of God" at some time in their future.[11]

Throughout the Old Testament, the sacrifice has a defined content. It is an admission of a problem and an expression of hope. The child of the woman, promised in Genesis 3:15, would make amends and conquer death and sin, just as the first animal killed by God covered the evidence of sin in Adam's nakedness. A sacrifice was therefore an acknowledgment of a certain reality before God, not a luxury or a decoration. The Book of Hebrews in the New Testament tells us that Abel believed God, took him by his word, and understood what sacrifice was all about. By contrast, Cain brought something quite pleasant, but without the content that should be represented in the offering. He thought to please God, but not to admit his need of redemption.

So he chose to remain angry and killed his brother from envy. God had told him to seek to do what was right, but he chose not to figure it out. He did not want to conform

10. Heb 11:4.
11. See Gen 3:21, 4:4; Heb 11:4.

to what his parents probably told the boys about God's work on their behalf. Abel knew what that was and chose his offering accordingly. Cain did not, for whatever reason in his own mind. God had even told him to watch out, for "sin is crouching at your door; it desires to have you, but you must master it."[12] Yet he refused and carried his anger out into the field to his brother, whom he then attacked and killed. There was no need, no master plan, and no evident purpose of God behind this action. It plainly states that Cain was angry and, though warned, made his choice. But his decision to follow through with his envy and kill his brother did not have to happen. It was neither necessary nor inevitable.

Imagine how hard it must have been for Noah to be different. His neighbors must have thought him odd as he stood out amongst them with his views and choices.[13] They laughed at and scorned him. His social and cultural context was so different from what he valued and practiced.[14] They took part in an undisciplined power struggle in a lawless social context and random efforts to survive. He grew up in hardship, in the midst of a family in which "labor and painful toil of our hands caused by the ground"[15] was constantly a reality. God had cursed the ground,[16] so that it now no longer simply provided for everyone's need.

After the Fall of Adam, the ground threatened survival by becoming a wilderness of thorns and thistles.[17] All

12. Gen 4:7.
13. Gen 6:9.
14. Gen 6:5, 12.
15. Gen 5:29.
16. Gen 3:17.
17. Ibid.

of nature was affected, and the relationship between Man and nature was now laborious, sweaty, and hostile. Nature was always there, impersonal, indifferent to human needs, harsh, and in constant need of being subdued. God had told the people that they must now put their hand to the plow and labor for a living.

Against the romantic notions of a peaceful life on the land, of agrarian societies, and of peasant culture, which we find in anti-industrialist romantic writers like William Blake or painters like Henry Fuseli in the nineteenth century, and among many urban dwellers in the twenty-first, reality is often quite different. In the immediate exposure to the details of the natural world, within what is otherwise and from a distance a majestic panorama of fields and mountains, people will encounter and have to address more cold indifference than wonder. Close-up, nature is untamed, at best an uncaring model for human behavior, at worst a cruel one. Yet, when people have no higher, personal, or more discerning viewpoint, they will take their cues for life from the animals around them, their closest living neighbors.

And animals function according to instinctual templates, not deliberate acts of love, respect, grace, and service. Animals do not love, do not speak, and do not make moral decisions. They mate, they signal states of being, and they struggle to survive.

I have lived for years in a village among neighbors whose animals were the most immediate models for behavior of living beings. Largely removed from the reminder of a higher calling, according to which we are made in God's image rather than in the image of nature, it becomes that much more difficult not to follow the surrounding natural model. It is easy to behave like animals in sexual mores, in limited communication, and in seeing a benefit where the competition of one more person is reduced and moral obligations are removed in the struggle to own one's living space. Compromise and understanding, which are building blocks for continuing human relationships in marriage and family, are hard to embrace when the final struggle is one of survival.

The impersonal universe around us does not furnish us with either instruction or specific models for a distinctly chosen moral life. It exists, but does not instruct morally. It can be described, but cannot prescribe anything in turn. Only in Scripture does one find a transfer of moral and practical insight from God who among the three members of the Holy Trinity said: "Let us create male and female in our image" and then made male and female dependent on each other in love, respect, and intimacy.

We read in the account of Noah's life and circumstances, that his father, Lamech, understood why life was so hard. "God had cursed the ground."[18] There is then a choice to be made. Either one accepts that situation as normal and sees what one can get away with, or one considers how one should live righteously before this God who judges, so that the curse does not become more severe and painful, and fallen nature does not get the last word. Noah's family chose the latter.

But most of the other people went the other way, with the consequence that "man's wickedness on earth had become" great. "Every inclination of the thoughts of his heart

---

18. Gen 5:29.

was only evil all the time."[19] When God therefore determines, "his heart full of pain," to wipe out the people he has made, Noah and his family are singled out, because "Noah was a righteous man among the people of his time, and he walked with God."[20]

Surviving the flood in the ark must have been a wonder. But even then, in the immediate aftermath, the survivors are reminded of the constant need for moral choices, lest they fall back into habits they will have remembered from before their rescue. God gives new covenantal stipulations, moral prescriptions, and a reminder of the fact that human beings are uniquely made in the image of God and worthy of special attention, protection, and admiration.[21]

Noah had made choices. He did not think or live like everyone else. There was nothing automatic or determined about his willingness to stand apart. He was one in the community of people, but not in the community of people's beliefs. He knew from his lineage and background that the ground was cursed, abnormal, and dangerous; consequently, moral choices had to trump political or natural choices.

The moral basis is found in the character of God, not in natural law or popular consensus. When he heard that he should build an ark, he started even before it rained. People laughed for weeks, but he persisted. When the rains came and rose and covered all the dry land, they drowned, but God kept Noah safe.

History could have gone another way. We do not know the specifics of another way, but understand the

19. Gen 6:5.
20. Gen 6:9.
21. Gen 9:5–17.

The Weight of Significance 63

amazingly consequential significance of Noah's choices. When we go back in our family history, figuring out where the family members came from, we can list few or many generations. But before we do that, all of us can already look back to Noah, who chose to believe God. Because of his choice to live differently, he survived, and we are among his descendants.

Later in Genesis, we read of the special promise God made with Abraham about becoming the father of a great nation, and that through him all peoples on earth would be blessed.[22] It is widely understood that this blessing from God would come through the Messiah, that child of a woman who would undo the reality of what Adam and Eve had done through their revolt against God. The reversal of the curse and all its consequences is the one central blessing all people need and desire. Johann Sebastian Bach's 1716 Cantata for Advent, translated as "Jesu, Joy of Man's Desiring"[23] expresses that only Jesus is able to fulfill the deepest longing, even when people will look elsewhere and will eventually be utterly surprised. Through the Messiah's work, all of creation will one day be made whole again. It is a fascinating story. There is a flow to history from then into our own days, and beyond.

At that time, Abraham had no children and must have wondered how that promise would become fulfillment in history. How would it happen? He had been tossed about in an alien land, had even gone to Egypt during a famine and had barely survived Pharaoh's discovery that Sarai was,

22. Gen 12:1–7.

23. *Herz und Mund und Tat und Leben* (*Heart and Mouth and Deed and Life*), BWV 147.

in fact, Abraham's wife, and not his sister, a story Abraham had invented to avoid Pharaoh's possibly murderous intentions by letting Pharaoh take Sarai into his harem. Both were now getting into advanced years; they had no children and Abraham understandably wondered how the promise would possibly be fulfilled. He mentioned this to God, as he feared that his estate would soon fall as inheritance to the family of his servant Eliezer of Damascus.[24]

God answered with a promise that Abraham's own son would be the heir. Through this son Abraham's descendants would become as numerous as the stars in heaven. Everything in the original promise would become reality through this one son, yet to be born. There was hope. The promise of God was sure. Abraham would not just be the last limb of a family tree. He would be the root of a tree with many branches in history. But when would this son be born?[25]

Sarai had not conceived a child before and was advancing in years. In light of this, she urged Abraham to sleep with an Egyptian servant, Hagar, in order to get this promised son.[26] A child was conceived in this liaison and a son was born, Ishmael. But was there a need for that breach of the marriage intimacy? Was this the way for Abraham to get to the first step in the fulfillment of the original promise?

Immediate results followed this indiscretion and haste. Hagar with her child now turned on and despised her mistress, who still had no child. Sarah, Abraham's wife, blamed him for having created this situation, though she

24. Genesis 15:2–3.
25. Gen 15: 4–5.
26. Gen 16:2.

had proposed it in the first place. Sarah in turn mistreated Hagar and sent her off packing into the desert. They had all made a great mess of their lives. Hagar fled to restore a semblance of peace in the home tent, but that did not last very long, as Hagar, forsaken by the father of her child, was told by an angel of the Lord to return and to submit to Sarah.[27] Of course, there was no real way back out of a situation that did not have to occur. Nothing was as it had been before. Abraham could have chosen to believe God and wait for the promised son. But he did not, creating altogether a very tense situation between the two women and, in the course of centuries of subsequent history into our own days, between the children of Ishmael and those of Isaac with their common father.

One wonders how history would have shaped up if there had not been Abraham's haste and urgency to have a son any which way. There would have been no Ishmael! And no common claim on Abraham by two very different views of God and the world.

JOSEPH IN EGYPT: CONTRASTING INTENTIONS

The Bible contains many such records of choices that did not have to be made. It makes the biblical text so accessible, speaking of real human situations among people like us. Real choices were made because people are free, have a will of their own to be informed and then choose how to act or not act.

---

27. Gen 16:4–9.

In the story of Joseph, it is plain that the brothers did not have to sell Joseph to the Midianites, a caravan of people on their way to Egypt. Joseph himself did not have to boast of his special relationship to his father. As a young upstart and child of Jacob's favorite wife, he showed off the colorful coat and boasted of his dreams of supremacy. But the brothers also chose to do away with him, either by murder or by selling him off to be carried away into a distant land.[28]

That account gives evidence of many choices made by each person, including the lengthy discussion among the brothers on how to proceed with their scheme. Even Reuben, who initially had his own design to save Joseph and to return him to their father, rather than to leave him prey to ferocious desert animals, joined the brothers' story. Together they used the convenient appearance of a caravan of Ishmaelites, another name for Midianites,[29] as a marketing opportunity. The brothers sold him off to spice traders on their way to Egypt. Together, the brothers then drenched the coat in animal blood to pretend their brother's misfortune of having been devoured by a ferocious animal to the disconsolate father.[30]

When many readers notice the summary statement at the end of the whole account of Joseph and his brothers in Genesis 50:20—"You intended to harm me, but God intended it for good to accomplish what is now being done, the saving of many lives"—they will be tempted to conclude, to their relief, that it was part of a good overall purpose. What started out as human wickedness was well

28. The account of Joseph's life starts in Genesis 37.
29. Judges 8:24, where both names are used interchangeably.
30. Gen 37:31–33.

worth it in light of the end result. That is the immediate, but perhaps too speedy and even superficial impression after reading the passage.

It forces us to remember and review what was laid out in my earlier considerations, especially in light of the suggested difference between the common embrace of fatalism and the unusual propositions in the Bible of derived human sovereignty. Is everything planned by God, so that nothing happened that was not meant to have happened? In this view history is indeed an unrolling of an existing blueprint, and our choices only appear to be real and historic. It makes history something inevitable, as God means everything to happen the way it does.

Let me give you the reason why I suggest just now that this is a hasty impression, rather than a careful consideration of the text. It fits into many people's hopeful reading of the many tragic events in a fallen world, but overlooks the reality of tragedy itself, in response to which you read of God's disappointments, of Christ's anger, and of the Holy Spirit's efforts to teach us and to remind us of all truths, because we are prone to forget them. If, in fact, from the outset all events were in any way intended by God as they occured, rather than foreseen (i.e. seen ahead of their occurrence) with sadness by an all-knowing God, they and any divine reactions to them would only seem to be something that they are really not. God would lose his moral credibility. There would be no room for real tragedy, sorrow, or judgment, as all events and circumstances in life would be understood as part of the same interlocked, unavoidable, and necessary history.

If God's actions and words only *seem* to be genuine, then they become in fact only lines in a theatrical play to be recited at the appropriate moments. That, in turn, would shape our understanding of God into what we may be familiar with from liberal theology and Eastern religions. Common to both schools of thought is the teaching that reality is not finally real, but only an appearance filtered through our mental categories for entertainment, and for our feelings and their psychological effect.

Many seek recourse in the suggestion of God's *accomodatio* to our finite minds. God's *accomodatio* means that things seem to us and are told us in words relative to our capacity to understand. But one should make the distinction between easy language and false language, between real events and fairy tales. The God of the Bible is unknowable and possibly non-existent, unless his words are true and the events real. The weight, charm, and wonder of the Bible are the continuity of meaning between what is true to God and true to man. The Kantian epistemological wall is neither necessary nor inevitable when one starts with the proposition that God is an eternal thinking, feeling, and acting person, who has made man in his image. Then, human categories are not producing error or appearances, but correspond to godly categories, from where they have their ultimate characteristics.

Reality is what it is, both inexhaustibly to God and comprehensibly true to Man. Our apperceptions do not distort God's perception. Tragedy, to us as people, is not our incapacity to accept the inevitable or divinely appointed. Instead it is the experience of what is contrary to God's intention in a world that does not yet manifest God's will. Jesus also was greatly distressed and wept![31]

When we return to the end of the Joseph story in Genesis 50, the question we still need to answer is this: How else, then, can we understand that verse about God's intention of all things for good? As applicable to all texts, whether contracts, love letters, or Bible verses, any statement must be considered in its immediate and wider context, to reflect on what it could, as well as what it could not possibly mean. With that in mind, I suggest that, from its position at the end of the "saga," it is a summary statement, somewhat like "all is well that ends well." And that it is not for reasons of giving an average evaluation, as one would say "all things considered."

Nor is it a description that every little component was a good thing. Paul writes repeatedly that we should be thankful in but not for all situations. In his letter to the church in Rome, Paul specifically says that "we know that in all things God works for the good of those who love him," but only after he says what those "all things" are: "the whole creation and we inwardly groan while waiting for the adoption as sons and the redemption of our bodies."[32]

This is a time of trial, but we are not uncared for. We object, but not as those who have no hope. God's intention in the midst of everything will bring about something far better. But not each experience along the way is the result of his intention, just as the Fall of Adam and Eve or the murder of Abel was not God's intention.

31. John 11:33, 35.
32. Rom 8:18–30.

When we fail to see this, we allow for the development of something like a divine *conspiracy theory* in the Bible. That term describes stories with supposed inside scoops, revealing hidden knowledge of forces or movers who plotted events. In the Joseph story, the conspiracy is that God advanced his causes by means of human wickedness. Like with all such theories, an attempt is made to connect the dots between what God did and what the brothers did in each situation they created by their wickedness. In this way, the theory or doctrine seeks to point to an order, a necessity, and a reason behind a frightening world of good and bad choices by a multitude of personages. It proposes a narrative of causation, when, in fact, the brothers make their choices, and God is not bound by them but counters them with his.

But if a conspiracy could be proved that the Joseph story was God's intention from the beginning, the brothers would not have been so evil after all. They would have merely played a role for some heavenly and moral purpose of God's intention. They would have only acted out what the heavenly prompter whispered them to do. In effect, they could then blame God for their ruthless wickedness.

This is the kind of transfer of responsibility all too common in Scripture and in our daily lives: Adam blames the woman God had given him; she blames the serpent which God had created, though as an angel; and Satan blames God for not wanting Adam and Eve to "be like God."[33] Yet much of Scripture is the defense of God against precisely this accusation of his originating anything in personages, in nature, or in history.

33. Gen 3:1–13.

Seeing history in the way so many see it, from Adam on down, would allow one to overlook the cruel and deceitful means by which the brothers acted to get rid of their youngest sibling, in order to be able to embrace the divinely intended ends.

Such a theory has everything go according to an original plan, though what such a plan contained is only ever discovered in hindsight.[34] The assumption is that what happened was intended all along. Such a theory prefers the security offered by belief in a closed system of necessary components, of a divine inevitability, to the untidy motivations and largely unpredictable actions of the brothers, and the sovereign, powerful, and moral responses of God *ex post facto*, after the sin of Man. It includes in its proposition the assumption that every event is the effect of a cause instead of a real choice.

But neither the action of the brothers nor the response of God to care for Joseph, in that miserable situation they had put him in, is an effect of just a prior necessity. Both are original choices of personages in a significant history: God acts and originates, as do people made in the image of the Creator. No choice is finally already caused.

Were all choices truly caused, there would not have been mandates for Adam and Eve to fill out or to obey, using their original creativity to name animals, to create their union, or to find ways to have dominion over creation and over themselves.

Adam's fall is neither an intended nor unintended consequence of God's choice to have human beings as part

---

34. Since God tells us quite a different plan of a good creation and harmonious human relations.

of his creation. It is in the nature of people, in their "kind," to be original and sovereign choice makers. *That* is what God intended for them. His intention was not specific to every choice they would make in Eden. God set the frame, the form, the setting; they broke out of it by believing they could "be like God." That is tempting in one's imagination perhaps, but oh so foolish!

On the background of that biblical teaching, the commonly assumed reading of Genesis 50:20 could surely not be concluded from either what the Bible tells us or what is meant with the given text in its larger context. Instead the verse sums up, at the end of the first book of the Bible, a real history of wicked choices by people, and God's intervention again and again to not have the wickedness of man win out and triumph. Joseph's brothers and some of the folk at Pharaoh's court thought they would have the last word and write the rules themselves. But God intends the final outcome, the good for his people, though it must often be achieved with special effort and against hindrances on the way, which are placed there by prior choices of men and women.

That is why the promised Messiah came not through Abel's line but Cain's, and why Isaac grew up with a half-brother, Ishmael. In the Joseph story as well, God would surprise everyone with his ability to produce a different outcome than they had tried to create. God accomplished that very well and put the brothers to shame! He breaks the bands of all determinism, any implied fates, and any hint of a closed system universe. Instead he affirms the reality of human and divine choices.

HISTORY'S PAINFUL MARCH

King David also faced a multitude of situations in which he could have chosen otherwise.[35] He did not need to go through every maneuver to hide his adultery with Bathsheba and finally send Uriah to the front in the war, to make sure he would be killed and not find out that Bathsheba was carrying David's child. Had he not gone that route in his own life, he would have been able to deal much more strongly with the members of his family, with the Amnon who raped his sister[36] and Absalom who openly conspired against David and mocked the king.[37] His choice made him weak as father and king. History records this; the Bible is no cover-up. But there was no need for this descent into greater sorrow due to sin. David could have repented instead of digging in, perpetuating his wicked choices, and loading one burden on another to everyone's detriment after him.

The story of Abigail's[38] choice also shows how history is made, not followed, how choices are not a program but an act of the will. She chose to step in when David had reasons to be furious at her husband, Nabal, for refusing to give some sustenance for his men.

Abigail stepped in as soon as she heard of her husband's insulting behavior toward David. She prepared to make up for his foolish actions. Without telling her husband, she and her servants gathered a large amount of food and drink and approached the camp where David and his men were.

35. 2 Sam 11.
36. 2 Sam 13.
37. 2 Sam 15–18.
38. 1 Sam 25.

By her choice, she prevented certain disaster to her whole family. That was an extraordinary thing that freed David from having to punish Abigail's husband. Her choice and its consequences moved David's heart and kept him from bloodshed that day.

Solomon, like all of us later, also chose to create a history that did not have to go that way. As David's son he received a conditional promise from God: The Messiah, that blessing to all nations through a woman in the family of Abraham, would sit on the throne of David, his father. Solomon would continue the line, if he remained faithful. To David, the promise was unconditional; to Solomon, it became a conditional promise from God.[39]

When therefore Solomon decided to take 700 wives in all manner of political marriages, for reasons of state and from personal interest, he failed to fulfill the condition. That was it. There was no need for these political compromises or marital arrangements. Solomon chose them. Had he remained faithful, the Messiah would have come through his line of descent. As it was, Jesus was born to the house of David, but not the house of Solomon. Another son of David, with the name of Nathan, became the ancestor of Christ the Messiah.[40] Solomon had a choice and failed. History ran on yet another track. We know one or two consequences, but God knows them all, down to our own days.

History also records what happened as a result of Jonah's various choices, including his preaching in Nineveh. Had he made different choices all along the way, events

---

39. Compare the different promises to David, 2 Sam 7:12–16, and to Solomon, 2 Chr 7:17–19.

40. 2 Sam 5:14; Luke 3:31.

would have turned out quite differently. As a result of his decisions, it took him longer to get there than it would have otherwise. Already on the way there, he affected people and situations.

Have you ever noticed the loss the sailors incurred when they had to throw all their cargo into the water? If Jonah had not decided to run away from God, they would have merrily made their way and traded as they intended. Now they had nothing but fear and dread. It became a wasted journey for them, filled with days of anguish and loss. They benefitted from understanding something about God, human significance, and judgment. Surely they now feared God and made vows and a sacrifice to him. They had been drawn into the whirlwind of God's dealing with Jonah for the sake of Nineveh and lost all they had but their ship and their lives. They did not suffer as a punishment from God, but the consequences of the sin of one of God's prophets burdened them heavily.

When Jonah finally arrived in Nineveh, thousands of the inhabitants of this great city repented and turned to God. They were saved from the announced destruction of the city and its people. That is indeed finally a wonderful and very positive consequence, affected by the choice of Jonah to respond to the lessons he learned when he had been thrown overboard to still a storm, was swallowed by a big fish, and spat on shore. At that point and after surviving such a great surprise, he chose to go where God wanted him to go in the first place. He preached and had an effect on many people's lives. The point of making those announcements of judgment had been achieved. People changed their ways and lived.

However, the initial choice to take the next boat in the harbor, wherever it was headed, rather than to find one that would take him closer to Nineveh also meant that he got to the city later than he would have otherwise. The three days in the belly of the fish also meant that his warning about the coming doom went unheard by all those who died during the delay before Jonah reached town. They had no opportunity to repent. They did not hear. They continued in their revelries and their belief that all was fine. Then they died, and they escaped the impending doom by death rather than repentance and still had to face a judgment they could have avoided had Jonah only gone straight where God called him to go.

History: people's lives and circumstances! It all occurs neither by itself nor because of some divine plan. Choices make a difference in the record of what did occur and what could have.

In fact, reading through the books of Samuel, Kings, and Chronicles, or any of the prophetic books of the Old Testament, or the letters to the confused, messed up, needy, and troubled churches in the New Testament, we are confronted at all times with real people like ourselves. Bad and good kings, false prophets and true, unfaithful husbands, and all too spiritual believers live in the reality of choices to be made or in the consequence of choices made by others.

There is no necessity for many of these events in the measure in which people are still free. Existing ties of the past and previous generations do constrain us in many ways. Yet even with that burden of the past on our shoulders and in our body and psyche, in our historic and geographic context, there is always an element of freedom, of a derived sovereignty, wherein we are called and able to make decisions.

There was no need for the bad kings in Israel's history or the many terrible governments in our own. There is no need to fall for religious charlatans, political idealists, false promises, or blind love. Most advertisements are exaggerations; many are deceptive. There is no safe world, playground, or schoolyard. No teacher is always correct, fair, and generous. No medical doctor can act as if he or she were God. Discernment, questioning, and a good bit of Cartesian doubt should be part of our approach to the real world before we make decisions.

For whatever we choose will have definite consequences. To avoid those we should reject, we need to recognize what power we have. For by our choices we create history, lives, tragedies, new inventions, time, safety, and all manner of real things. Our children will look at that and wonder why we chose some of them, even though there was no necessity for them.

Much could also have turned out differently, if only . . .

PERSISTENCE AGAINST OBSTRUCTIONS

Imagine what would have been the result of Mary, the mother of Jesus, being unwilling to be the mother of the Messiah? All kinds of thoughts might crowd into your mind. But they are ideas from your rich store of imagined, *what if* alternatives, which of course never materialized. But it is no idle game. In fact Luke tells us how Mary responded favorably to the angel's announcement. It was a choice she made and had to make. It was not a decided thing. Mary's question, How would this come to be since she was not yet married to Joseph?[41] receives a detailed answer. It was not

---

41. Luke 1:34.

a question based on a rejection, but she still had to agree. Francis Schaeffer spoke often of the need for what he called "active passivity" as exhibited in Mary's reaction[42] to the angelic announcement. God would conceive in her a body for the Lord, but she had to agree to become the Lord's "handmaiden."

Yet she could have chosen to hesitate or even to refuse. In which case, history would not have come to a stop, but God would have announced the conception to another virgin among those who waited for such a time that one of them would bear the Messiah in fulfillment of the earlier promise of God's blessing to all nations.

In the same vein, we know from Scripture that Jesus came to "do the Father's will." He frequently announced to his disciples that he came to die in Jerusalem, once they understood that he had come to initiate his kingdom. At times we find them not understanding this intention; at other times they speak and work against it. But he was steadfast in pursuit of his present purpose. He did not remain with them on the Mount of Transfiguration,[43] though Peter, John, and James suggested that as a neat idea: Jesus already in glory, the three of them on top of a mountain, resting under the booths they had assembled there. They would be away from the damaged people and broken world all around them.

But instead Jesus did what Moses and Elijah had also come to talk to him about: his coming departure;[44] his death on the cross; his suffering insult, pain and humiliation, and

42. Luke 1:38.
43. Matt 17:1–9; Luke 9:28–36.
44. Luke 9:31.

The Weight of Significance 79

a real death physically; and his real separation from his Father, morally and theologically.

The most comforting thing about all this is that Jesus also dreaded that hour and wished that he did not have to go through it.[45] It would not be surprising to find out, eventually, that Jesus did have a real, existential choice in the matter of his reaction, first, and then in his going through with it. The fact that it was God's will did not in any way diminish the reality of repulsion Jesus expressed and his need to actively choose to "do the Father's will." If this were not so, the words of agony would be only the recitation of lines in a script. The whole work of Christ would be theater, not a life. The cry on the cross, "My God, why have you forsaken me?" would be poetry, liturgy at best, but no genuine indication that God had in fact forsaken the eternal Son of God, who had become "sin for us on the tree."[46]

History would have gone quite another way, and it would continue in a different direction, if Christ had not chosen to go on to face and experience all that Jerusalem was throwing at his face, body, and being.

Even Judas in the end did not have to proceed the way he did. As in all situations with personal beings, choice is involved on some central level. Judas was not a pawn in the plans of God, no victim of a greater purpose, imprisoned by the need to have someone betray Jesus to Roman authorities and to Jewish scorn and accusations.

Judas was the disciple who betrayed Jesus for thirty pieces of silver. But we must also remember that all along

45. John 12:27.
46. For this image, see Gal 3:23 and 1 Pet 2:24.

he seems to have had a problem with money.[47] The betrayal was not the first upsetting event, though it was the most consequential. Judas had objected to the jar of ointment being poured on Jesus' feet, for the money could have been given to the poor. He had kept the money of the group in his bag. We do not know for certain whether that was the final or even central motive of Judas. We also know that prophecy in Zechariah foretold such an event.[48] We read in the text that Jesus knew who would betray him. But none of that diminishes in any way the choice Judas had, for none of these circumstantial factors necessarily diminishes the central affirmation of Scripture that personages have and do make a choice at all times.

The Bible creates and reflects the mentality born from its specific view of the world. It leans strongly against the thinking that history is the determining principle and power behind human action or that God as sovereign diminishes or violates the real freedom of human agents. We find such genuine freedom described in Scripture—for instance, when David attempted to hide in the city of Keilah from Saul's pursuit.[49] David's reaction to the announcement from a knowing God that citizens of Keilah would hand him over to his enemy, Saul, made it impossible for the events to ever occur. For David of course ran away. Thanks to God, David knew what would happen if he sat still. So, not being a fool, he ran away from what God told him would happen, and so, as God already knew, it never happened.

47. John 12:4–6; 13:29.
48. Zech 11:12.
49. 1 Sam 23.

TEMPTING TIDY TOTALITARIANISM

By contrast, Stalin, as a materialist, thought and acted in a way that saw people as part of the means of production of a new mankind. People and machinery would come together like gears in a machine to produce what he envisaged. There was a strong determinist perspective, unlike the scriptural view of the real freedom people have to choose. Plato also suggested squeezing people into their required role in the *Republic*, for the sake of the greater good of all. Choice should be eliminated, as it creates an open, untidy situation far different from the desired tidiness of a closed system in which people are denied their derived sovereignty of choice.

The search for a tidy solution is not found only in distant philosophies. It occurs whenever we deny the particular in favor of the universal, whenever we think in stereotypes instead of persons, whenever we reduce complex realities into closed systems, which can be political, cultural, and theological. It is far easier to look at everything controlled by God, Allah, or fate, than to recognize that the God of the Bible created an open creation and history. It was and remains unfinished, open to new thoughts, actions and inventions, historic events and failures, and genuine repentance. It also remains open, waiting to bring about what God has promised to yet do in times ahead, when he will make all things right again and death itself will be swallowed up.

The embrace of a tidy program view without unfinished business promises relief from uncertainties. That is its attraction, its charm, its selling point. Uncertainties are precisely what we fear. We much prefer rest and resolution. We are uncomfortable in decisions yet to be made relating to choices about our future, work, and marriage. But only the sovereignty of chosen initiatives makes us persons and gives evidence that we are in the image of God, the creator, and are thereby real people. Too readily, we are prepared instead to commit to utopian proposals of resolution, views that offer closure, an order without the choices yet to be made, the ground yet to be covered, and the space yet to be filled.

The pursuit of utopian ends always requires the "minor sacrifice" of your individuality. Large numbers of people, minds, or money are run over in order to accomplish the intended greater end. In Stalin's case, it amounted to 60 million dead. Hitler sought to achieve the purity of a race, for the improvement of mankind, by similar means and vicious programs. Many schools of Islam demand the sacrifice of female intelligence for the benefit of family and society. Most religions, in fact, require the believer to "just believe," which means to not question and discover, but to accept and follow. They require that a person abandon normal and necessary curiosity and inquisitiveness about the content of the faith, how it relates to the givens of the real world, whether it even relates to the real world rather than some spiritual play, smoke, and mirrors. It is a form of faith in faith, rather than a faith in facts at hand. The Bible speaks about believing God to tell us the truth about life and reality, about him and us in the context of a created and defined world with an accessible history to be wisely chosen each day.

Instead, both religious and secular faith tends to be a finished view, a kind of utopian idealism, a totalitarian vision that is then imposed on what is otherwise a very complex reality. It is an attempt to reduce all reality to a single focus, a link between a single unified cause and its effect. By contrast, the Bible does not even have that focus in God, who reveals himself as Trinity, from which a harmonious variety descends into creation. The eternal one, God, is himself both unity and diversity. There is a dynamic of love in the specific Godhead, a give and take, an unfinished-ness, a continuous pleasure of each person of the Trinity in the others within the moral character of God. That is the background from which we understand how Christianity and biblical Judaism have refrained from seeing life as a representation of monopolistic tyranny or multi-polar anarchy.

As I suggest in *The Innocence of God*, at greater detail, even divine providence sees ahead (Latin: *providere*) but does not in all cases approve every aspect of what is announced. Creatures also contribute to the outcome. This does not make prophecy vague, couched in mysteries or other forms of epistemological uncertainties. Instead we, the creatures, can retard or advance, even prevent at times, what is surely foretold. The Israelites did not enter the Promised Land when initially promised. They all had to wait until the older generation, which did not believe God, had died. Therefore, instead of the foreseen 400 years, which Abraham knew about, it actually took 430 years for the conquest of the land promised to Abraham.

For, to the God of the Bible, history is real, not a program of necessity! Events, choices, alternatives, all weigh in and contribute to what happens at any time. God's foreknowledge includes not only what will happen, but also what could happen, if only . . . ; and what could never happen, even if . . . !

How weighty our choices are, for good and ill, we will consider in the next chapter.

Chapter 4

Weighty Consequences of Our Choices

For such reasons, history is a record of things that happened, and also of what did not happen, because of a determined choice by a person. I want to show you what I mean in the following considerations, which have nothing to do directly with events in relation to the Bible or Christianity, except where all relates to choices people made, just as the Bible records real people in real time.

In a recent airing of a PBS program[1] on the air war against Germany, much was made of the difference between the U.S. intentions and those of the British allies. London, through an error in navigation and bad weather, had been bombed only partially on the nights the German planes approached the island. Revenge in kind, but avoiding a similar mistake, became the strategy of the English. Carry the war to the city of Hamburg itself!

America had a different strategy. Its purpose was to starve and destroy German industrial production and thereby bring the Nazi regime to its knees and the war to an end. The British bomber command wanted the civilian

---

1. http://www.pbs.org/thewar/detail_5213.htm.

population to be so harmed that they would rise against their government[2].

The distinction was maintained for many months. British bombers firebombed Hamburg, Berlin, and other population centers. The Americans flew in their craft and dropped their bombs on such targets as rail yards and the ball bearing factory of Fichtel & Sachs in Schweinfurt.

The reasons behind two divergent strategies were clearly stated. For all those months, Americans were reluctant to harm civilians. But then a choice was made to

---

2. Conrad C. Crane wrote on the PBS site: "Sir Hugh Trenchard developed tactics and policies for the world's first independent air service and when talented subordinates such as Hardinge Goulburn Giffard, 1st Viscount Tiverton (subsequently 2nd Earl of Halsbury) pioneered target analysis for morale and material effects to assault the foundations of the German war economy. Although airmen in both countries became aware of the ideas of Giulio Douhet during the interwar years and used them to support arguments for strategic airpower, Douhet had little impact on the evolution of the RAF or the U.S. Army Air Corps.

The RAF continued to pursue Trenchard's ideal of a massive aerial offensive, assisted by politicians who were willing to fund an aerial deterrent instead of large expensive land armies that could become involved in more bloody continental wars. However, targeting priorities remained vague, and the war would soon reveal the large gap between claims and capabilities.

The Americans took a different approach that can be traced back to Tiverton's precedents. Although the subordinate army air service's primary mission remained ground support, a group of smart young officers at the Air Corps Tactical School (ACTS) developed a theory of precision daylight bombing of carefully selected targets in the industrial and service systems of enemy economies. Pinning their hopes on the capabilities of new aircraft such as the B-17 Flying Fortress, these airmen expected unescorted self-defending bombers to destroy vital nodes of the enemy's war economy that would grind it to a halt".

change the strategy, as so often in history. A different course of action became acceptable and necessary when increasing numbers of U.S. bombers did not return, and the losses became too heavy. Late in the campaign, American generals added fighter planes to their sorties and joined the British in targeting civilian areas as well, until the end of the war.

But it was a distinct, deliberate choice with different consequences. There had not been a master plan from the beginning. Instead, two divergent views of war, civilian populations, and attitudes about enemy countries existed until they were merged. Who but God knows what that change produced, what would have been the length of war had the merger taken place earlier? Who would have died or lived, if the other strategy had prevailed?

Perhaps it is the impossibility to answer those questions that drives many people to seek a good reason and a larger purpose for whatever did or does happen. We do not like to be left with the loose ends of a *what if* question, which only God is able to answer. We only know, at best, what happened. We do not know what would have happened, if . . . Contingent situations remain strangers to us.

TOO SOON FOR CLOSURE

Yet the drive to find an answer, a resolution, or closure is strong in each of us. We do want to know, even if only to know what we missed or how lucky we are. It is a kind of attempt to attach the drifting boat of our life's experiences to the shore of (even imaginary) certainty.

We want to relate to a larger context, a world in which we are at home and which would explain our individual experience as part of a larger scheme of things. The meaning of the word *religion* sums up this effort to relate. It is not a sign of childish discontent or immaturity. Gauguin writes the basic human question on the canvas of his famous painting: "What? Whence? Whither?"[3] Duerkheimer suggests that religion comes out of the sensation of our enclosure in a family, a tribe, a nation, which limits our self-centeredness by drawing us into a fellowship with rules about respect, assistance, and submission. From the awareness of such rules, one deduces a rule-giver, an ancestor or a god.

Atheistic worldviews also see individual people tied to something larger than a single life. At times the image of a river is used, in which everything is carried along the river's path, like autumn leaves floating in the current. History is seen as a story between the start, "once upon a time," and the anticipated conclusion, "and they lived happily ever after." That arc of progress, from uncertainty and possible tension to resolution, is also present in Marxism, which borrows from Hegel and relates all people and events to the inevitable scientific progression of history through conflict towards a final harmony. Religions unify, attach, and place the particular life into the context of a universal, a unity of Being, a whole One.

From the biblical perspective, human beings relate to the person of God, an eternal being of specific, limited attributes in infinite measure: God as holy, specific, distinct, infinite in his specific being, but not infinity as such. He is someone who thinks, feels, and does. He has made men and women in his image to likewise be persons, though finite

3. In the Boston Museum of Fine Arts: "D'ou venons-nous? Que sommes-nous? Ou allons-nous?"

ones. Yet over against this Creator, our present situation is flawed, imperfect, and not as originally intended. Something drastic happened between creation and now. There has been the Fall of Adam and Eve, as I mentioned above. Written history looks like a continuous story, but in fact, real history became what it always is: far more chaotic.

While the longing for more, better, and more fulfilling situations is common to everyone, only the biblical description of the real world gives an explanation of the background of the present conditions and mandates to create, to work against their rule over us: to impose culture on nature, both on the impersonal stuff around us and on our own human nature, and to act morally, rather than politically. By that I mean that what is right, rather than how to get by together, is to be our pursuit.

Without that biblical perspective, nature is the final horizon and stage, the first and last thing we see every day, the dominant theme that surrounds us, and the place where life unrolls. Religions embrace that natural scenery, while Christianity found a different text. It speaks first to the mind, rather than the body, and needs to be understood, rather than merely recited. It answers basic questions coherently and enables us to promote a life reflecting the image of God. Without it, nature is indeed the ground we walk on and the firmament that covers us.

For example, Plato, looking at the night sky, describes in *Timaeus*, in the form of a dialogue, his account of the origin of the visible world from that vision of permanence. Plato's mind and his recent experiences in Athens craved an order, a logical and practical way to resolve uncertainties of events and human conduct. Aristotle delighted, instead, in the regular motion from potentiality to actuality of all things in nature. Each thought they had found in these regular patterns the essential character of the universe.

That regularity in the firmament above and in nature around them gave them the model of what society should adopt for it to be orderly, and for the individual to know his place in pursuit of virtue in the larger scheme of things. It is not surprising, then, when each philosopher proposed a model for people and society. Plato took the examples of eternal passages of heavenly bodies, Aristotle the steady motion of natural processes.

The effect would be, according to Plato, a harmonious program of a State and its citizens, and according to Aristotle, a society modeled on nature. For the sake of an ideal order, Plato "disallowed" artists and poets with their troubling lines, provocative ideas, and unpredictable and disturbing influence over the citizens' minds. For a similar ideal order, Aristotle demanded of people a conformity to virtues modeled on patterns observed in nature. He subsumed people's moral concerns to political ideals. From an urgency to fit in, people were expected to give up and to avoid such "extremes" as moral judgments.

The pursuit of either ideal of conformity came with a price—no more independent thought, creativity, and personal responsibility. They were buried in the interests of the polis as a whole. Greek tragedy and a generally fatalistic outlook in Greek culture made it easy for many later idealistic, totalitarian cultures to refer back to Greece as their model.

Other societies also found their integration either in things of heaven or earth. They looked to the control of stars, or the seasons of the year, or the fertility of the fields and forests. Surrounded with the uncertainties of life, they sought shelter in adjusting their views to what happened in the visible world around them.

Only in the small, Jewish cultural context on the eastern shore of the Mediterranean do we find an alternative to such a system orientation. The God of the Bible describes a very different relationship between individuals, and between them and God. The contrast could not be more exceptional. This model shaped a culture of responsibility, personal conscience, innovation, and repentance, of which we are heirs with our present worldview. It did not arise spontaneously, nor does it continue with a life of its own. It requires from us constant effort and affirmation. Without it, we likewise will slide into patterns of life that are more marked by resignation than by purposeful exhibitions of moral courage. The difference of JHVH[4] and the difference he makes to our outlook are well stated with the contrast between fatalism and initiative, between entrepreneurship and resignation, between history as a prison, and time and space as a playing field.

Athens had undergone violent civil war, chaotic popular democracy, and rivalries among oligarchs and archons. The search for a harmonious interplay between Man and nature, the state and the soul of Man, and layers of society had become a major concern for Greek thinkers and poets. Gradually they sought to replace an often immoral pantheon of contradictory divinities in Homer's writings with something more stable. A system of justice, logical consistency,

4. These four letters are the tetragram of Jewish Scripture, to which added vowels give the pronunciation "Jehovah."

and social harmony was preferable. At first such order was suggested by pre-Socratic philosophers in Asia Minor to lie in impersonal elements, or what are described as, in the words of some modern philosophers, "grounds of being." They suggested water, air, fire, and a boundless everything. Plato sought the stability in eternal forms, models, or permanent ideals, which he believed to exist outside our circle of transient existence.

Applying these forms to reality would make the shadows of particular shapes and events on earth somewhat more real, and would thereby bind society and virtue to a belief in absolutes beyond the ups and downs of current troubles. An appeal to eternal and perfect forms, to ideals, gets rid of opposition, but also of vibrant discussions and cultural vitality. When the ideal is assumed and the perfect is already known, nothing is out of place, inferior, or in need of improvement.

The results are habits of repetition rather than innovation. When it is believed that we already live in the best of all possible worlds, challenges no longer exist. Life is then reflected in patterns, rituals, and community. This leaves no room for any prescriptive challenge or openness to what might be new, better, and liberating from the closed system of repetitions. There are no invitations or challenges to create variety. The unfinished, untidy reality of the human and natural context is overlooked or removed. *Culture* is reduced to what people already do, not what should be done, to address the boredom of repetitions. Birth and death, love and violence: everything is part of the social interaction, without an outside evaluation.

Yet that is what Noah did, when he behaved differently. He believed the God in heaven, which gave him the critical distance from outside to reject the common.

THE DREAM OF ORDER IMPRISONS PERSONS

This appealing source of order, constructed on the foundation of ideas drawn from an eternal perfect form, was unfortunately assumed by Alexandrian Christians like Origen and Clement. In it they saw an indication of how close the pagan Plato was to the Christian understanding of God. Eager to link their view to the world of Greek thought around them, they gave away the meat and became intellectual vegetarians. Their apologetic became an apology. They failed to make the weighty distinction between permanent ideals of *love* and *justice* in Plato's view and the consistently loving and just God of the Bible and unrolling history. Plato's forms are permanent and static, while God is historically continuous and dynamic. God is not justice as an ideal, but is always, in every new situation, just. We are called to seek justice in situations, not as an abstraction. Justice, like the Sabbath, is to serve people, rather than the other way around.

Subsequently Plato's forms or ideals, with their projected light and power on the wall of our observable history, have been widely accepted as a good halfway understanding of God. In Christian thought, Plato's forms have become God's sovereign rule, a divinely controlled history that is at all times willed by God. History as manifestation of eternal forms, in Plato, is now history as the expression of the will of God. Plato's idea of imagined forms above our temporal reality has been altered into a God outside of sequential decisions and acts.

This adjustment to Greek ideas does God and us an enormous disservice. The God of the Bible is not an ideal, a form. He is the Eternal Person: engaged, enterprising, purposeful in sequential acts. He does not hide in moral and intellectual mysteries, but came as Lord and Savior to go before us.

We should remember that the embrace of abstract ideals, such visions of perfection, has become, according to Karl Popper, the justification of multiple totalitarian political and religious systems. Visions of a pure race, of an egalitarian new humanity, of an exclusive religion, of tolerance as an absolute, variations of nationalisms or a pre-industrial "nativist" world, have been pursued up to our own days at the cost of enormous bloodshed. Whenever idealism has been imposed on society or sought between people, the result has been totalitarianism and the destruction of what is at least possible.

That has also happened with the idealized God and his sovereignty over all of history in the view of many Christians. I say this as strongly as I do for a reason. If God is in such sovereign control over history, moral considerations about what is done by Man or devil no longer weigh in. If God is pleased with what happens now and is in no way troubled, as is the case when everything now runs according to his will and plan, he has no moral character.

This would be a perfect "form" of power, but not of integrity, of will, but not of moral distinctions. It is the idea of perfection that people find so attractive. Many are willing to give up their moral sense for it, to embrace mystery as an answer, rather than to end up with the unfinished business of a world that will remain untidy until the day God sets all things right.

The image, the "imagination," of perfection is as appealing a substitute as the golden calf was for the God of Israel at the time of Moses and Aaron. Here is a striking parallel that reveals a common mindset. In their impatience, the people filled the absence of Moses on the mountain with a sculpture of the holy cow, or golden calf, made from their precious melted jewelry.[5] They had been given that gold by Egyptians, when they were leaving Egypt.[6] Now they turned it into idolatry! The pursuit of totalitarian idealism is similarly impatient and perverted. It removes the messiness of an untidy, real, and present world, with its signs of unpredictable individuality, of thought or discussion, and replaces it with the comfort of immediate and total conformity. It overlooks the particulars of people, of moments in time, and of incomplete efforts, in favor of a universal vision of harmony, resolution, and totality.

Stalin, Hitler, the prophet Mohammed, the leader of the Khmer Rouge Pol Pot, at times the Popes in Rome, and more recently a multitude of Protestant quasi-popes, want their people to fall in line. They prefer a controlled, repetitive, and aligned public, where the perfect is already known and nothing is out of place or inferior. Threats of hell or the sword may have to enforce compliance with the ideal. Human opinions on every possible subject are hailed as God's intended instruction, to be followed in order to

5. Exod 32: 2–4.
6. Exod 12:35.

achieve perfection in families, education, business, and politics.

The results are habits of repetition, rather than innovation. When it is believed that we already live in the best of all possible worlds and own final insights, challenges and doubts no longer exist. There are no invitations to create variety or to make improvements, to learn from mistakes, to reconsider, and to adjust to different contingencies. The actually unfinished, untidy reality of the human and natural context is denied. Culture is reduced to folklore, faith to bits of affirmation, and politics to positions on the right and left. The sharper focus is on following, repeating always what people already do and believe instead of weighing what should be done to address the boredom of repetitions and to relieve the pain of the wounded.

Father Stalin, Hitler ("who had such a warm way with children"), and Mr. Kim, North Korea's dictator, share the fame of having given their people an ideal, finished, perfect, impersonal culture under a "great leader."[7]

CONFORMITY THROUGH MONOTONOUS REPETITIONS

I mentioned above how normal it is for children to attach themselves to the world they grow up in. They are inexperienced; their minds are still developing. They are initially alone, insecure, and unable to relate to the various events

---

7. "Only to the survivors, not the exterminated," I pointed out to the mayor of Rostov-on-Don, when he referred to Stalin's popularity and his own acclaim as the single candidate in local elections. He had, I mentioned, no way to know whether people voted for him from love or fear.

and impressions they face. Conformity to something or someone in the immediate world outside (ourselves) brings confirmation, comfort, and, eventually, a sense of belonging in community. Hence the importance of culture in its modern definition, whether it is in the form of rites of passage or folklore or international food-fests: it is what is already and habitually done by a group of people.

Rest in, and familiarity with, such habits, rites, and formulae are offered to each individual as a kind of religion. In fact such is the fundamental nature of all transcendent and immanent religions, whether they are secular and naturalistic or spiritual and revealed religions: each person seeks to relate to something bigger, of longer duration, of greater weight than himself. They satisfy a person's initial need to fit in, to go with the approved and traditional, in order to avoid alienation and isolation. One's personal world is too small, one's experience too limited, one's need for care and protection, for explanations and repetitions, too urgent to remain "outside" on our own. We expect answers as food for our minds quite soon after we have instinctively expected food for our bodies. Warmth, protection, and, eventually, conversation make us experience "belonging," a sense of being at home in the human race.

We relate, with obvious benefit, when we learn the vocabulary of our family, the meaning and innuendoes of the words, the figures of speech, and the metaphors of the people around us. Only through adjustment to their social patterns and behavior do we understand and communicate adequately to find the way for life to go ahead.

However, we must gradually acquire the tools to become independent, to notice distinctions, and to resist blind conformism. A more mature person's attachment will become more critically discerning and seek out something or someone more reliable than the world and authorities he first encountered. The critical distance helps us to balance attachment with increasing individuality. We relate, but are not absorbed. We become links in a chain, rather than part of an iron rod. We maintain our unique diversity within the unity of a common language.

Diversity becomes more difficult, if not eventually impossible, if we attach ourselves to whatever is assumed also to direct the world in the bigger questions. Here, too much conformity implies diminished uniqueness. The careful balance between unity and diversity, the one and the many, the permanent and the variable, is easily lost. In Islam, one is obliged to accept the orders and the perfect will of Allah. In African tribal religions, as John Mbiti points out so well, the authority of the ancestors and the power of the spirits determine life and behavior in colorful variations.[8] History is the energy behind the inevitable progress in Marxism and the dialectic in materialism, which determines one's place and obligations through struggle at every turn of life. The material conditions of a person induce his behavior. The material weight of the stars and their position in the firmament above weigh on a person's personality and ordain the outcome of their marriage.

Buddhism calls for increasing disciplines of denial in order to lose oneself in the undifferentiated *one* of Being. According to Zen teaching, man enters the waters and causes no ripple on undifferentiated oneness. Hinduism suggests a fundamental justice in the way the die is cast for

8. See Mbiti, *Religion and Philosophy*.

the Karma of a person's position and life experiences, his caste and circumstances.

In Greek thought, the fates direct what people experience. There is nothing that Electra could do to escape the impending judgment. All things are controlled, determined, and inevitable. Antigone has to die for reasons of state, for reasons of the gods, and of "necessity." German soldiers would later die for that of heroism.

Plays like those of Sophocles present us with a culture of fates, heroes, revenge, and death, all in a closed system of necessities. Greek ideas have also permeated the teaching of the church for centuries. The Christian Roman senator and author Boethius had translated many works of these Greek philosophers into Latin and was intimately familiar with their view of the world. Plato's eternal forms and Aristotle's Unmoved Mover behind all nature in constant motion became the lenses through which he understood Christianity. His major work, "The Consolation of Philosophy," was translated and widely read after his death for a thousand years in the Western church.

We remember that when Boethius was falsely accused of an intrigue involving the Senate in Rome against the Western Roman Emperor he found his consolation for the injustice, the false accusations, and finally his death in the teaching by an invented personage, Lady Philosophy. But she comforts him with ideas from Plato and Aristotle, rather than the Bible and Christ. She suggests that all things and events come from God and must therefore not be bad, as God would not want to harm you. Consequently, the experience of pain and false accusations show up due to one's flawed perception, not flawed events. We are familiar with such an interpretation in aspects of both hard Calvinism and Buddhism, both of which teach, in various ways, that any problem only exists in your mind and perception, but not in the real world outside.

Your way of thinking about evil has to change, not the evil itself. That change of viewpoint will remove the present pain, which means nothing anyway at present in light of the coming eternity. Belief that God would not allow anything bad makes Boethius conclude that the bad things must in fact be good. He now longs for death, to be free from the burden of temporal agony, and thereby adopts a further Greek idea. Boethius adopts the outlook of Greek heroism, where the goal is death, rather than a justified life.

These are not views found in the life or teaching of Jesus. Instead such a view reveals the Gnostic denial of the real material, historic, rational world. The focus on faith, spirituality, and mystery makes any real history seem to be a shadow of Plato's eternal forms, rather than the stuff in which Jesus chased out the moneychangers from the Temple. In fact, any actual moral distance between what people do and what God wills is denied. It makes history and the tragic, unjust, and in the end deadly events in the life of Boethius an expression of the perfect will of God.

On such a smooth run, all reality results from the original creation and is subsequently sustained alone by the grace of God. Nothing really upsetting happens afterwards. The cart is made and the apples are forever safe on it. There is no evidence that the Bible's creation format—i.e., there is a real world functioning according to nature's laws and real people who make good and bad choices, make an effort, and at times fail—has any relation to this.

Instead, all of life is not necessarily or "naturally" so. The Bible actually talks about the world we are very familiar with. It is a world where the apples roll all over creation and into the gutter when the cart gets kicked over. In Boethius's world nothing is out of place. How then does he understand the anger of Christ, who, according to Scripture, was not part of what naturally happened to people, but rather wanted to change their lives and their world?

The efforts throughout the life and teaching of Jesus Christ deal always with each particular result of sin and death. It is all very painful to him and is met with authoritative intervention from the Son of God.

Boethius's Lady Philosophy was admired throughout much of the Middle Ages and the then Christian church. Whenever a peculiar understanding of divine sovereignty requires believers to accept all events and disturbances as justified and fulfilling God's will, even Protestant orientations have been affected by this classical Greek notion of life being ruled by fate. The only difference from Greek or Islamic determinism is that a benevolent purpose is thought to exist even in the most hideous tragedies and injustice. "God's sovereignty," separated from the complex record of human choices, becomes a lens that blacks out the reality spoken about in the Bible and encountered in our daily experience.

The materialist, with his particular lens, does not admit the personal and supernatural in the real world. The divine determinist eliminates real human significance.

Both schools of thought are reductionists with a simple, one-dimensional perspective. They bring their own presuppositions to the text and to real phenomena or to what is happening in history. Both are also idealists with a single center, focus, and energy that determine all outcomes. In the end, their outlook is totalitarian: Either matter or God determines everything. Genesis 1, where God creates and then mandates the creature to do the same in his and her imagination, is not preserved. Nor is the genuine rivalry of Genesis 3 admitted, when Adam and Eve fall for Satan's tempting proposition to become like God.

In the reductionist perspective of history, all events are seen as unrolling according to a materialist or a divine plan. In that case, nothing in history could have been different and all events inevitably occurred.

NOT HIS FATHER'S WORLD

The view laid out is widely held. I propose, however, that this is not what the Bible teaches and certainly not what we find exhibited in the life of Jesus. When Jesus is introduced by some to have come to share our suffering, to model submission, and to accept what happens as necessary in the plan of God, his character and mission are distorted. For the Jesus revealed in the Bible is more like Christ the Tiger, an interventionist who confronts a fallen world with authority. He roars like the lion in the book of Amos against the sin of Man in the fallen world. He argues with Pharisees, heals the sick, drives out demons, forgives sin, and conquers death itself. He is no pacifist, but fully engages in the battle for which he came, and goes on to defeat sin, guilt, and death.

Fatalistic views produce cultures of the "again and again," symbolized by the wheels of fate and the dictates of gods that rule without awakening a conscience or obliging us to compassion—life is seen to be controlled by necessities. Things happen because they are meant to happen.

This view is widely held today, but is certainly not what we were taught from Scripture in the past. The Bible awakened believers to engagement, critical analysis, and courage to seek improvements. We should be startled in our minds and driven to action (which is correctly seen as typically "Western"), when people accept the fate and suffering of their neighbor in other cultures. Death, disease, and cruelty stir us to action and resistance because we assume them to be abnormal, undeserved, and avoidable.

We are troubled and rightly concerned about attitudes widely held in African tribal contexts, Indian slums, and among Bolivian *campesinos* or peasants. Unfortunately we find them also in the "black stocking" Calvinist environment of parts of Europe. There, a particular view of Christianity agrees with the modern scientific reductionism to a closed system view of reality.

A newspaper reported that a young man was knifed by two others on a station platform in the midst of a crowd of other passengers for refusing to hand over his cell phone. No one interfered or helped. In a world where nothing can happen that is not in some way deserved, planned, or sovereignly ordained, no wrong or evil ever really exists either. "He must have in some way deserved it," and "He had it coming to him," and "It was his fault, he should have handed it to them," were the defensive comments at the time. They were products of a view that everything is in order, nothing is really wrong, for we all get what we deserve. Not in an end judgment, mind you, but now already!

Weighty Consequences of Our Choices

Yet the Bible speaks of a world now out of line, unfair, and unfinished. The judgment is yet to come. It is not always, and never fully, found in what we experience now. "The ungodly who prosper in the world"; "the tents of the marauders are undisturbed, those who carry their gods in their hands"; and "wherefore does the way of the wicked prosper?" are profoundly accurate descriptions of the present abnormality, not of the will of God.[9]

With such a view, nothing can be admitted as being unnecessary, wrong, and evil. History is, in that perspective, a record of what needed to happen, what was meant to happen, what was unavoidable, as if someone gave it that meaning. It assumes a just world, a determined reality, a necessary sequence. Nothing is ever really out of place in it, except of course the occasional person who, with a rare case of moral sensitivity, does not smooth things over, refuses to grant forgiveness as a way to feel better about himself, and regrets the "passing" of others, whose life he would have preferred to last longer. If only there were more of such persons!

The price for belonging or relating to such a bigger "whatever," whether matter or God, is not just the abolition of personal uniqueness, creativity, and enterprise. It also demands the denial of moral discernment, though it does not prevent judgmental pronouncements about other people. Characteristic of each one of these attachments is an assumption that the reality is already final, that everything is in order, that the case is closed. There are no more hard edges and sharp corners. There are neither distinct moral categories nor specific tasks to accomplish.

9. Ps 73:12; Job 12:6; Jer 12:1.

Problems arise only from the presence of a mind that stands outside the collective, the fate, and the necessity, and looks at them with a moral, critical, and discerning perspective. A mind, in other words, that has not concluded that whatever is real is all there ever could or should be. Such a mind comes alive from the obvious contrast between birth and death, between distinct individual personalities, and between the multiple contradictions encountered in a life, from a deceptive or illogical use of language, to promises not kept, to death as a violation of everything one previously struggled for in life.

Such a mind, such a person, thinks, evaluates, discerns, and complains. This mind understands that a remedy or improvement of a painful situation can only come through repentance, imagination, and enterprise. This mind leaves the circle of "that's just life," in order to bend life into a different shape. Jesus came to manifest such a mind in the person of God. He taught that, and he calls all people to follow what God has said, rather than what the silent history of the universe exhibits.

Plato's firmament is impersonal, cold, and distant; Aristotle's nature is amoral and silent. Looking around us, at the stars above or the flowers in the field below, can serve as reference only at the expense of our becoming less than human ourselves. But the child of God follows a living person, not an idea. Only a living God can inform human beings to turn a damaged history away from the rule of blind necessity.

RESOURCEFUL MORAL PEOPLE

Moses and Deborah in the Bible have taken such a different stand from moral resourcefulness. Others have followed their example, from similar insights, into the nature of reality under the God of the Bible. Moses, Jeremiah, Job, and many others in Scripture take their cue from God, not the world around them or an idea about it. We can add Ezra, Nehemiah, and Esther to the list of people who by their singular choice and at times clever efforts move their neighbors, other Jews, and dwellers in the land to stand up rather than to submit, to change the flow of history in a different direction, by their moral, intellectual, and practical choices. Because of the contrasts they experience in that real world, they argue, raise questions, and oppose any form of blind submission.

Moses notices the contrast between the covenant that God made with the people and the regrets God expresses when they become rebellious in the wilderness.[10] That raises questions and leads to an argument with God. It also brings out Moses' moral reaction to step into the breach. He intercedes for the people and holds God to his promises. Thereby he changes the moral weight of the situation and God's relation to it. It is not that Moses "saves the day," but he refuses to accept a historic situation as final. God always encourages each of us to make history, with our contribution to it, something else than a normal flow of events.

Only an infinite person with an accessible and defined character can be the standard and confirmation that being a human being is not a cosmic mistake. The creator can ex-

10. Exod 32–34.

plain what he created! Significance is not an illusion. That is the view the Bible reveals to us. History demonstrates the reality of it. People come alive and struggle for better things when they realize what events in history occurred neither from necessity nor a divinely appointed inevitability. Both experience and explanation come together as a tightly fitting match.

It comes as no great surprise when cultures with an intellectually closed sky above them, or given only nature's indifferent and often morbid model around them, will be blind to greater possibilities of confronting and reducing human suffering. Man's mind and heart require as much intellectual insight, moral orientation, and personal motivation as the body needs food and protection. When the mental/spiritual areas of our lives are not awakened and nurtured, the result is often material and cultural poverty from intellectual darkness bound up with religious mysteries.

In such a world, the human being becomes an accidental phenomenon, somewhat of a misfit. The difference between animal and human being is essentially the latter's mind, by which he thinks, imagines, and determines how to distance himself from the haunting pursuit of natural hardships. We survive mostly by thought and learning, not by physical strength or instinct. Man's longings for answers, encouragement, and good ideas are not met when he has nothing more as neighbors than an impersonal, and therefore uncaring, nature, time, and deadly fate. We need reasons to object to the normality of a painful life. Without them we are much more likely to accept everything as inevitable. In such a view history is a record of tragic and possibly funny stories. They relate what is normal, even what is painful and unfair. This record contains no moral compulsion, no mandate to do anything. Everyone simply always gets what comes his way. He may just be at a certain place at a certain time, and there is nothing wrong about it. It is just an inevitable occurrence.

Such a view was widespread in Europe's past, under Greek and Roman influence. It is widely current in other parts of the world. Where the Bible's teaching has not been understood philosophically, even formerly Christian cultural contexts return to a fatalistic outlook, created by both scientific reductionism and, in another extreme, by a growing fascination with esoteric powers. The former abandons the reality, the latter the necessary control of the mind. There are similarities of irrationality between pagan fear of spirits and the influence of a charismatic version of Christianity.

The views of the Greek/Roman world came through the teaching brought to the European continent by Jewish-educated apostles starting in the first century. In what way their lectures, sermons, and discussions changed a whole way of seeing the human being in the world will be the subject of the next chapter.

Chapter 5

History in the Seat of the Accused

The picture of the human being always the victim of circumstances and of higher powers, such as fates or gods, is found in our cultural context only where a fatalistic view has been adopted. Otherwise we largely live still under the influence of the teaching of the Bible. In the past, that Bible lifted us from such a view, when all we had was nature and its forces as our "habitat." The preaching of God's word, from Genesis to Revelation, enlightens us to seek wisdom from God, not from what already is and seemingly has always been: neighbors, the ups and downs of natural events, and the cruelty of life.

That instruction brought to light a high view of people, of work, of love, and of law as parts of the social fabric, and of a rational inquisitive mindset to know the nature of God's creation. It created a mentality that was deposited, like an inheritance for future generations, in minds and hearts, in libraries and buildings, in the very language itself. Our generation still draws interest from that investment. In so far as we do not renew that understanding and mentality, we will gnaw on the capital itself and may soon exhaust it.

Paul preached for only three weekends while he was in Thessalonica.[1] With his teaching, he totally changed the outlook they held, their Greek worldview, and the way they understood Man's place. He summed it up well at the end of the first section of the letter he wrote to the church in that major Greek city. He was made to leave in haste to avoid the persecution his words had enflamed.

As a consequence of his teaching, some inhabitants turned from (many) idols (of their own invention) to the one true and living God. They broke with the cyclical view of human history and now placed in God their hope of a different tomorrow with eternal life, since he had raised Christ from the dead. They also began to look at life differently. They saw their life experiences no longer a matter of chance and divine, absurd playfulness, but came to understand that they lived in a moral universe with a judgment of God waiting to address, deal with, and set right all that was so unresolved, unfair, and contradictory in each person's life experience.[2]

That is a very different view, one of an open history yet to be formed even in the midst of the limitations that do exist from past choices. We do not have total freedom, as if we were the first kids on the block and could still decide which way the roads run or where to beat a path over time across the young grass in the park. No, the city is there, the grid of the roads is laid out, the property boundaries are fixed and registered. There is a fence around the park.

1. Acts 17:2.

2. You will find a longer discussion of the content of Paul's teaching in Thessalonica in my book *Christianity vs. Fatalistic Religions in the War Against Poverty* (Colorado Springs: Authentic/STL, 2008).

The reality of our condition is perhaps best described using two old philosophical concepts. These are form and freedom, the givens and the possibilities in reality. When we stress either one more than the other, we make a mistake and get into trouble. Abandon the form and nothing is stable; abandon the freedom and the world of the mind, of thought and imagination, is an illusion.

The Portuguese, rationalist philosopher Spinoza saw the world as total form. Nothing could be altered, and freedom only existed in a mind willing to accept, rather than reject, whatever happens anyway. No one was free to object, to resist, or to do something else. Everyone had one choice and only one: you either got stuck or went with the flow; you experienced reality as a prison or you sat in your cell and sang, danced, or shouted. But in the cell you were. Your choice was to approve of it and not but against it.

That is a deterministic line of thinking. Whether the world, matter, or god functions that way, there is finally no real freedom, for everything merely follows a closed system of push and shove variations. Everything is in a real sense *one*. It only appears that possibilities exist.

The other emphasis is on freedom. It assumes that we are always at the threshold of the unknown and able to start something, regardless of prior conditions. We can play original creator and be a surprise to ourselves and others. A child will have that view in limited areas and consider that he is a magician in the world around him; with every smile, the child gets the adults to respond favorably. Yet, such freedom does not really exist, as the response to the child is in turn chosen by the parent. The child has not really determined the new situation, but he has laid the groundwork for it.

More realistic is the affirmation that form and freedom come together in an attempt to understand the human situation of each of us. The world is a given, we are born into a defined reality, but within certain limits we can give it shape, add to it, or destroy part of it. The limits are specific in our gender and age, our mind, and our body strength. But now, what are we going to do with them? That is up to you and me.

There is another limitation that already exists for each of us. We do well to realize that, even when our cultural context pretends the limitation is not that binding. While we can freely choose to create history, to spend money, to make babies, and to annoy friends, no one is able to do all these things and then pretend that there are no consequences. We are not free to have our cake and eat it as well.[3]

If that is a rough and simple description of the real historical situation, of our parameters, we should resist any temptation to assume, here, total form or total freedom to define our place. Neither alone does justice to our reality and experiences. Neither the material or religious determinist (by whatever label he identifies) nor the libertarian (with his own label again) reflects the real world even approximately. The former cannot live with his view each time he praises or blames someone or something, or in other ways wants to be taken seriously. The religious outlook about divine determinism is contradicted by prayer to change things, by commands to do things differently, as well as by deliberate acts of kindness and evidence of generosity among people.

---

3. The French equivalent proverb is, On ne peut pas avoir le beurre et l'argent du beurre.

The latter, the libertarian, will also protest, as when his children or spouse decide to become liberated, go their own way, and denounce his selfishness and that of others by way of justifying and then living out their own.

Christianity lays the foundation for a balanced view of form and freedom. History is indeed done in the past; the record is closed (even if not totally known to any of us). But the next moment's choice is still open, fully known only to God, who also, however, has not experienced it, until it happens.[4] Much could also go another way. Planning to do one thing is different from actually deciding to do it. There is real freedom, the rightful use of it and/or the failure in it. The knowledge of God ahead of time does not determine the outcome. For God's infinite knowledge does not only include what will happen but what would happen if another choice were made, and also what could never happen, no matter what was decided.

It is indeed a terrific thing to be so significant. It is terrifying: we can make a poor choice with much harm down the road. For that reason, it is not astounding that so many people are attracted to a deterministic view of things: fate, genetic makeup, a controlling historic context. If my choice can be linked in hindsight to God or economic and psychological reasons, I am reigned in like a horse by a bridle or a ship held by an anchor. That way the choice becomes what "is meant to be:"

---

4. It is interesting to observe that to God also there is the reality of "not yet" or conditional situations, as when John says that the Holy Spirit was not yet given, because Christ was not yet glorified: John 7:39. See also John 20:17.

History in the Seat of the Accused 113

I cannot fully be blamed. It was steered, not born from individuality. In fact a constrained act is no real choice at all, and I am not to be blamed!

A justification through hindsight, by looking back and lining up the determining ducks in a line, does give the impression that all events had to occur. It is a way of seeing the end first and then looking for the means. Voltaire writes in Candide:

> Il est démontré, disait-il, que les choses ne peuvent être autrement; car tout étant fait pour une fin, tout est nécessairement pour la meilleure fin. Remarquez bien que les nez ont été faits pour porter des lunettes; aussi avons-nous des lunettes.[5]
>
> (It is shown that things cannot be otherwise than as they are; for as all things have been created for some end, they must necessarily be created for the best end. Observe, for instance, the nose is formed for spectacles, therefore we wear spectacles.

Of course, that illustrates Voltaire's cynical enjoyment of an absurd backwards reasoning process in the church, which he objects to on intellectual and moral grounds. He defies the reasoning of those who saw God's hand in the earthquake of Lisbon and the terrible wars on the Balkans in the seventeenth century. He rejects the notion that every effect has a deliberate purpose, a single divine cause, which would serve as a justification for the effect that shapes the next decision. But he also ridicules the reasoning that just

---

5. Pg 3, Jean-Marc Robin, published by Lulu (2009) ISBN 978-1-4092-7118-5

because something happened as a result of a cause, the cause was therefore just.

The Bible gives a significantly different reading that matches the real situation more accurately. Looking back we recognize that every effect has a cause; otherwise nothing would happen. But the cause itself was often not a necessity but a choice.

The creation format, i.e., the fact that real world functions according to laws, applies fully to things and personages. What distinguishes us from plants and animals, from trees and rocks, is not random lawlessness. There is a law to our nature as much as there are nature's laws. Such lawfulness in nature prevents absurdity and indefiniteness and allows us to understand things and people. It makes science possible and enables us to come to explanations through rational procedures.

The difference between personages and things is not law and freedom, for both are defined in law; there is, however, a difference, which needs to be put at the right place. We notice that it is in the nature of personages to be free, whereas things and impersonal animals function according to their template. Our template, the law governing human beings, is to make choices all the time. The structure of natural things makes them function according to their program, with hardly a detectable exception. Our structure as human beings is that in most situations we want to be praised, because we made a choice and an effort, and we wish to escape the blame when we are wrong. Things cannot do otherwise, while we human beings need to be told how to do right, to seek justice, and to love our neighbors. They have no freedom to do otherwise, while we seek and treasure our freedom. They have no ideas of alternatives, while human beings are full of them, whether from rich imagination of good and bad goals or from anxiety that we are different from the material world around us. They have no choice about how to dress, while human beings change the fashions to our delight and, at times, to other's surprising gaze.

JESUS OVERTURNS THE TABLES

Alexander Pope presents yet another idea as his view of the universe. It is an attempt to find a middle ground between human sensitivity to wrong and pain and a belief in a good, finished product of creation without a fall having damaged what God had made.

He says that no matter how imperfect, complex, inscrutable, and disturbing the universe appears to be, it functions in a rational fashion, according to the natural laws. The natural laws consider the universe as a whole a perfect work of God. To humans, it appears to be evil and imperfect in many ways; however, Pope points out, that this is due to our limited mindset and intellectual capacity. Pope gets the message across that humans must accept their position in the "Great Chain of Being," which is at a middle stage between the angels and the beasts of the world. If we were able to accomplish this, then we potentially could lead happy and virtuous lives. One detects a possible influence of Boethius on this way of thinking.

"Essay on Man" is an affirmative poem of faith: life seems to be chaotic and confusing to man when he is in the center of it, but life is, according to Pope, really divinely ordered. In Pope's world, God exists and the universe is centered around him in order to have an ordered structure. The limited intelligence of man can only take in tiny portions of this order and can experience only partial truths. Hence man must rely on hope, which then leads into faith.

Pope's view has nothing to do with the biblical view. It is much closer to Boethius's Platonic aromas. He suggests that our mindset sees evil where in the bigger scheme of things there is none. He denies both real evil and the sensitivity of intelligent people to it. He ends up suggesting that faith serves as a cover-up, not the confidence of things hoped, the certainty of things not yet fully seen.[6] A genuine understanding of the Christian faith is a trust that God will keep his promise, an acceptance of the accuracy and relevance of God's view on a broken, damaged world that needs an extra effort on God's part and man's to be fixed.

Pope's view states well what is also found in much of what is called the "Reformed faith" by many contemporary pastors. They also advocate that the objectionable evil is all in the eye of "the beholder," in this case "the believer." For, it is said, in the providence of a sovereign God, all events are a necessary link in the chain of what in the end will be seen as the perfect work of God. Now it all seems wrong to men and women; but it only seems that way, while in God's reality it all fulfills God's purposes and should therefore be accepted in trusting faith. Let me suggest again that this view is much closer to Eastern mysticism than to what Scripture tells us about the character and life of Jesus. He came in the flesh to show us the opposite, i.e., that evil is evil, that not all problems are deserved, that Herod was a terrible king, and that the reasoning of the Pharisees had no foundation.

6. Heb 11:1.

History in the Seat of the Accused 117

Just because in hindsight every effect has a cause and every event streams forth from a prior cause does not justify the proposition that all events at present and into the future have already been caused. That every effect can most often be explained by looking back has a logic and rationality to it, which is appealing. That offers a measure of security, but it takes away a moral evaluation. It creates factually necessary links that are free from moral weights. The deed is done, the effects are as expected. The cause is known. Someone made a choice, and now it is too late for moral restraints. Yet any "indulgence in the sirens of retrospective determinism"[7] is not warranted. Future choices are open and will be morally judged!

According to the Bible, reality not only manifests the presence of God's grace, but also the effort by creatures, at times through repentance, then again by obstinacy and amazing creativity, for both good and evil. The freedom to act according to the nature of free agents is also assumed and stated when laws, commands, and exhortations are given to us. They point out that the wrong ideas a person has (e.g., to be "like God," to assert power, to despise another person, to appropriate someone else's work or pay) can be carried out, but they conflict with the real world's fundamental internal rationality. They are a lie, a sin, and a distinct disruption of the lawful functioning of the real world.

Such laws cannot prevent foolish ideas or force us to bow intellectually and morally to the shapes of created reality. But they shed light on what ought and ought not to be done in light of the way things are. What happens is then a choice, informed hopefully from an effort to have dominion

7. A wonderful term by Tony Judt, *Postwar*, 627.

over ourselves and our ideas, as well as over the surrounding world, with attention to both sets of laws: those which govern the real world and those which are moral prescriptions from God to govern our minds.

Or we neglect it all and pretend that we can create a world independent of reality, first in our minds and then by our actions. Such is the nature of dreams and the implementation of an ideology.

Sin, in the Christian context, is what is foolish and wicked in reality. In the reference to the Triangle Shirt Company fire in New York, the ladder on the fire truck was too short. For the sake of greater profit over the workers health, the control over their bathroom pauses is made absolute. In the fire 146 of the workers die, because what was imagined was not adjusted to the nature of reality!

How tragic, then, when a widely used ideological and theological filter of Christian determinism renders all events purposed and meaningful. The fact of its occurrence is seen as evidence of an underlying purpose, as such a filter assumes a morally and factually closed system between God's various wills ("permissive," "moral," or "perfect" will) and visible outcomes. You will recognize that such a view is much closer to a Platonic order, derived from his notion of eternal forms, and Aristotelian order, found in the wholeness and interrelatedness of all natural motion.

In philosophic terms, Christians who embrace such considerations have moved their theology from Jerusalem to Athens. For in the Bible, we discover a God who pleads with people to not have history become the instructor for their, our, moral orientation. We should discover the mind of God, not in the course of events, but in the text, in the

Word who became flesh and effected events dramatically, in opposition to the powers that thought to control them.

Only when we allow history to be a partially uncharted stretch of road ahead of us can we maintain the substantial distinction between necessary and contingent, good and evil, right and wrong. When there is no real choice involved, every situation is already approved, inevitable, and necessary, because all actions are understood to be in some form determined, either by natural conditions and circumstances or by the work, will, and purposes of God. When all of life is seen as flowing from the ubiquitous "grace of God," the platonic fatalism of Boethius's faith will be the result, undermining any constructive intervention, search for alternatives, and moral objection in bad situations.[8]

Bernhard Schlink, author of *The Reader* and *Guilt about the Past*, writes of such a loss of moral discernment when, in a relatively easy, diplomatic, and all too common embrace, all happenings are accepted and, thereby, the concern for actual truth and justice, and in the end even reality, is avoided. This is the case whenever the outcome is more important than the way to it, when the end justifies the means. For Boethius, the anticipation of heaven makes all injustice not only bearable but unimportant, quasi nonexistent. For Schlink, the acceptance of a colleague into a professional association is manipulated through flowery speeches and voting maneuvers, through sentimentality, instead of through disarming and removing false accusations, against very serious opposition. Boethius is pleased

---

8. Not so in *True Grit*, the film by the Coen Brothers. They insist on justice to undo, not to revenge, evil, while the musical theme plays many renditions of "Leaning on the Everlasting Arms."

with himself, but Schlink openly carries within him the thorn left behind by moral compromise.

In my view, Boethius commits the greater wrong. He compromises the moral nature of God, whom he has smoothing over all present evil in light of eternal perfection.

The Bible speaks of an untidy, not smooth, world, and of God's frustrations with what wrong choices have done to his rich and beautiful creation and to the relationship between Creator and creatures. We find that text to make moral distinctions between what is and what ought to be. It gives commands indicating that we need to choose between life and death. There are intervals and distinctions in prophetic fulfillment between the "already" and the "not yet" and "until," between the "atonement for wickedness" in the first coming of Christ and the "everlasting righteousness" yet to come on his return.[9]

For history is "the story of everything that needn't have been like that."[10]

With the alternate view, the system functions without missing a beat and is never belied by experience. Without a frown of doubt on his forehead, Eliphaz in the Scriptures suggests to Job a correlation between his pain and suffering, and guilt.[11] Nothing can disabuse Eliphaz and his friends of this. They cannot see someone distressed, struck down, without at once thinking he is like that justly. They assume a tidy world of fairness, of order. When they attack their victim, they

---

9. See Dan 9:24 for the two-fold promise of the Son of Man's work.

10. James, *Cultural Amnesia*, 15.

11. One of Job's three "friends" who assume that suffering is an indication of deserved punishment.

History in the Seat of the Accused 121

never have the least doubt that this victim is guilty. They do nothing else but apply that universal magic, causality, so well defined by the ethnologists, scientists, and moralists. In their view, they transpose onto Job something fairly common to animal life, wherein one cannot see a fellow creature injured, sick, or handicapped, in some way or the other, without attacking it, in order to rid the species of it.

That is neither the tenor nor the teaching of Scripture. It is the opposite view to the one found in certain primitive tribes where, when a death or a sickness strikes, a search begins for the one who is guilty, and who, when discovered, is disposed of. I knew parents who hid their handicapped child because outsiders "naturally" believed that the child was a punishment from God! Such views assume a normal world, without the fall and its effects, without sick persons, without infirm people, without sufferers, and above all without innocent people wrongly condemned.

Job's friends assume such a just world and express what is common outside of Jewish and Christian thought: the universal tendency to consider this misfortune as merited.

Against this Job rightly calls out:

> Even now, in fact, my witness is in heaven,
> and he that vouches for me is on high.
> My friends scorn me; my eye pours out tears
>   to God,
> that he would maintain the right of a mortal
>   with God,
> as one does for a neighbor.[12]

---

12. Job 16:19–21 NRSV.

Job speaks up to show that it is necessary that God himself take charge and play a role contrary to the one imposed on God by Job's friends. God must become the defender. If God would make himself known, he could defend Job. Yet, rather than Job's voice being an isolated human voice, it expresses in fact what constitutes the best of human effort: choice, and refusal to bow to circumstances. History is not self-promoting, self-mobile as time and sequence are by themselves. History is created through choices, both for good and for bad.

RESPONSIBLE MORAL ACTIONS

A powerful evidence for this understanding and its consequence is present in the reality of science, politics, and the arts. It is a human effort to understand the workings of the natural world of data and to make use of it in the choices open to each of us. Science would never have developed if humans had persevered in the belief of Job's friends, if they had continued to persecute victims each time someone suffered misfortune among them. They would never have caught a glimpse of the great biblical project, from which came forth the modern will to improve the human lot by all sorts of developments—scientific, technical, judicial, political, social, et cetera. These developments demand that divine causality be given its biblical limitation and that magical causality be renounced. People would never have invented medicine, for example, if, faced with the sores of Job, they had persevered in the idea that he was justly punished and that it would thwart God's will and judgment to try to heal him.

The Gospels do not establish humans in enterprises economic, scientific, artistic, or whatever. They have several other concerns. They cannot do what they do for victims, tyranny, or boredom without removing first the obstacles that, until then, impeded any development. There would have been few without much improvement of life (as much as there has been) if people's outlook had not first been changed and informed by the gospel outlook. The Gospels, in the context of all Scripture, cleared the way for belief and repentance, for action and hesitation, for enterprise and objection: in short, for a moral mandate to choose life over death, whatever ugly manifestation the latter would have.

Today we are, perhaps more than ever, in a position to understand the extent of the terrible evils mankind has created and inflicted on others. The savage blindness of the scapegoat mentality portrayed in Job's friends and the many ways of controlling people's religious and ideological belief is weakening, where the Bible and the Gospel begin to clear the view to a more accurate and human reading of existence. A measure of human freedom is gained by the release of mind and emotions from pagan religious bondage. That allows many to succeed in eliminating or attenuating evils that previously appeared to be without remedy. They had been imagined to be the work of some cruel deity or, amounting to the same thing, of some implacable nature or totalitarian or utopian ideology.

We are learning more and more to delineate and to master such evils. We are healing the sores of Job under the light of the Gospel's affirmation. The beginning of the good news is given in Mark's Gospel on the background of our awareness of the bad news of history.[13] The same phrase—"in the beginning"—tells of creation and of the additional work God undertook to have the Word become flesh for our redemption by way of a substitutionary sacrifice of Christ's real body in Jerusalem.[14]

It has surely required long centuries to obtain many results. I know well that very great evils have simultaneously come upon the scene, but they witness by the same token to a continuing liberty among human beings. The Bible and the Gospels are not responsible for the human abuse of what people have given to the world. In other words, both the increase in evils afflicting us and their diminution vindicate God, revealing the finally human origin of these evils. They are a constant challenge to human beings in their quest to live out the mandates, given at creation, to have dominion over oneself and the world around them. The first leads to moral responsibility, the second to moral action. Once human beings escape the theology of Job's three friends and recognize the authority of Jesus Christ and what he taught, they can attempt to begin to master the necessary means, if they only have the will to do so.

Such a freedom of the will exists where we are addressed as choice-makers, not imprisoned under a divine plan or a cosmic closed system. Choices are real where neither necessity nor an absolute ideal are the first and final reality. In the encouragement of making choices in recognition of real differences between good and evil, and what is reasonable and what is irrational, with benefits and damages as consequences, we come alive as people, to fulfill

13. Mark 1.
14. Gen 1:1; John 1:1.

History in the Seat of the Accused 125

the mandate to be creatures in the image of the Creator. Life is not a boring, colorless conveyor belt of events, but like a field to be planted. People are called to vary life's situations[15] and to put the hand to the plough against the thorns and thistles that threaten life after the fall of Adam and Eve.

History is always a record of things that took place. While many acts and much information will bring regret, many others we can be glad for. Unlike John Irving's way of arranging imaginary people in his novels to produce the final paragraph, to be the conclusion he had in mind all along, Christians and Jews in real life see characters as real people with decision-making abilities. They will not be pushed and shoved or molded into performing what is needed for the intended paragraph or line at the end, at some future point in time. Instead, God's compassionate and creative powers will so act that without "violence . . . done to the will of the creature" God's intentions will in the end be achieved. What may take additional time and effort, come through delays and creative interventions, overcome obstacles and human foolishness, will always be a part of history.

History remains, then, a record of things that were neither necessary nor inevitable. They did not have to take place, but did. You and I also have choices to make to ensure that what we will add to the record is not quite as foolish, destructive, or unwise.

Our children at first, and certainly one day also God, will check out how we have done.

---

15. How clearly, and with what delight, did Adam not realize that Eve was like him, of his kind, totally unlike the animals he had just named: Gen 2:23, 24.

Bibliography

Bacon, Francis. *Novum Organon*. New York: Cambridge University Press, 2000.

Boorstin, Daniel. *The Seekers: The Story of Man's Continuing Quest to Understand His World*. New York: Random House, 1998.

———. *The Discoverers: A History of Man's Search to Know His World and Himself*. New York: Vintage, 1985.

Gibbon, Edward. *The History of The Decline and Fall of the Roman Empire*. Vol. 3. 1781.

Haberman, Clyde. "Choosing Not to Forget What Is Painful to Recall." *New York Times*, 26 March 2010, A19.

James, Clive. *Cultural Amnesia*. New York: Norton, 2007.

Judt, Tony. *Postwar: A History of Europe Since 1945*. New York: Penguin, 2005.

Mbiti, John. *African Religion and Philosophy*. Garden City, NY: Norton, 1992.

Middelmann, Udo. *The Innocence of God*. Colorado Springs: Authentic/STL, 2007.

www.ingramcontent.com/pod-product-compliance
Lightning Source LLC
Chambersburg PA
CBHW072145160426
43197CB00012B/2250